GREAT
GARTER STITCH

by Jean Leinhauser and Rita Weiss

STERLING

New York / London
www.sterlingpublishing.com

Produced by

Production Team

Creative Directors
Rita Weiss and Jean Leinhauser

Senior Technical Editor
Ellen W. Liberles

Technical Editor
Rita Greenfeder

Photography
James Pape
Carol Wilson Mansfield
Marshall Williams

Fashion Stylist
Christy Stevenson

Pattern Testers
Kimberly Britt
Patricia Honaker

Book Design
Graphic Solutions inc-chgo

STERLING and the distinctive Sterling logo are
registered trademarks of Sterling Publishing Co., Inc.

Library of Congress Cataloging-in-Publication Data Available

10 9 8 7 6 5 4 3 2 1

Published by Sterling Publishing Co., Inc.
387 Park Avenue South, New York, NY 10016
© 2008 by The Creative Partners™ LLC
Distributed in Canada by Sterling Publishing
c/o Canadian Manda Group, 165 Dufferin Street,
Toronto, Ontario, Canada M6K 3H6
Distributed in Great Britain by Chrysalis Books Group
PLC The Chrysalis Building, Bramley Road, London
W10 6SP, England
Distributed in Australia by Capricorn Link (Australia) Pty. Ltd.
P.O. Box 704, Windsor, NSW 2756, Australia

Printed in China
All rights reserved

Sterling ISBN 13: 978-1-4027-2308-7
        ISBN-10: 1-4027-2308-3

For information about custom editions, special sales, premium and
corporate purchases, please contact Sterling Special Sales Department
at 800-805-5489 or specialsales@sterlingpublishing.com.

INTRODUCTION

What is garter stitch?

Well, it's a knit stitch, followed by a knit stitch, followed by another knit stitch—for row after row! Sound dull? To many knitters, garter stitch is indeed boring. In fact garter stitch is sort of the ugly step sister of stockinette stitch in the mind of many.

But garter stitch actually has many dimensions. You can use it to make lace, bobbles and borders, cords and curlicues, colorful mosaics, flowing ruffles, charming intarsia designs, ripples and waves—and much more.

In this book you will see garter stitch in a whole new light. These pages are filled with tempting designs, fascinating stitches, and unusual techniques and textures. If you'd like to create your own garter stitch projects, we even give you a collection of over 30 different versions of garter stitch in our stitch section starting on page 107. So come along with us and discover how the humble knit stitch can be used to create knitting magic.

And believe it or not, there's not a single word called "purl" anywhere in the book!

Jean Leinhauser

Rita Weiss

CONTENTS

TOASTY WARM HOODIE

Designed by Nazanin S. Fard

*Zip up in this hoodie
and keep out the cool
breezes. Easy-to-make
and easy-to-wear,
this will be a wonderful
addition to any wardrobe.*

TOASTY WARM HOODIE

SIZES	Small	Medium	Large
Body Bust Measurements	30"- 34"	36"- 40"	42"- 46"
Finished Bust Measurements	40"	44"	48"

Note: *Instructions are written for size Small; changes for sizes Medium and Large are in parentheses.*

Materials

Bulky weight yarn

17.5 oz variegated

Note: *Photographed model made with Bernat® Galaxy #53110 Neptune*

20 (20, 22)" separating zipper

3 stitch holders or waste yarn

Stitch marker

Size 10 1/2 (6.5 mm) knitting needles
   (or size required for gauge)

Size J crochet hook

Gauge

10 sts = 4"

Stitch Guide

M1: Insert needle under the yarn between the stitch just made and the next stitch and twist it. Knit in the twisted yarn loop.

INSTRUCTIONS

BODY

Starting at bottom, CO 100 (108, 120) sts.

Knit every row for 14 (14, 15)" from CO edge, ending by working a right-side row.

Divide for front and back: K25 (27, 30) sts for right front and place on a holder, knit next 50 (54, 60) sts for back, then place last 25 (27, 30) sts on holder for left front.

BACK

K50 (54, 60) sts for 10 (10, 11)" more until piece measures 24 (24, 26)" from CO edge, ending by working a right-side row. Place all sts on a holder.

RIGHT FRONT

Sl right front sts from holder onto knitting needles, attach yarn and continue knitting for 6 (6, 7)" or until the piece measures 20 (20, 22)" from CO edge, ending at front edge.

NECK SHAPING

BO 4 (5, 5) sts at neck edge, knit across: 21 (22, 25) sts.

Row 1: Knit across.

Row 2: K1, SSK, knit across.

Repeat rows 1 and 2, 3 (3, 4) times total: 17 (18, 20) sts.

Continue knitting until piece measures 24 (24, 26)" from CO edge.

Using 3-needle technique (see page 126), BO 17 (18, 20) sts from right front shoulder with 17 (18, 20) sts from back shoulder leaving rem center back and left shoulder sts on holder.

TOASTY WARM HOODIE

LEFT FRONT

Sl sts left front sts onto knitting needles, attach yarn and continue knitting for 6 (6, 7)" or until piece measures 20 (20, 22)" from CO edge, ending at front edge.

NECK SHAPING

BO 4 (5, 5) sts at neck edge, knit across: 21 (22, 25) sts.

Row 1: Knit across.

Row 2: K1, K2tog, knit across.

Repeat rows 1 and 2, 3 (3, 4) times more: 17 (18, 20) sts.

Continue knitting until piece measures 24 (24, 26)" from CO edge.

Using 3-needle technique (see page 126), BO 17 (18, 20) sts from left front shoulder with 17 (18, 20) sts from back shoulder.

HOOD

With right side facing, pick up and K16 (15, 17) sts from right front neck edge, K8 (9, 10) sts from back neck holder, place marker, knit rem 8 (9, 10) sts from back neck holder, pick up and K16 (15, 17) sts from the left front neck edge: 48, (48, 54) sts. Knit for 4". M1 on each side of the center back marker:

For size **small**, inc every 8 rows 4 times: 56 sts.

For size **medium**, inc every 6 rows 4 times: 56 sts.

For size **large**, inc once: 56 sts.

Continue even in garter st until hood measures 14 1/2". Knit to center marker. Fold hood piece in half and using the 3-needle bind-off technique, BO all sts.

SLEEVE (Make 2)

Starting at bottom, CO 22 (24, 26) sts.

For size **small:** Knit every row, inc one st each side every 3 rows 6 times, then every 5 rows 8 times: 50 sts.

For size **medium:** Knit every row, inc one st each side every 3 rows 6 times, then every 6 rows 7 times: 50 sts.

For size **large:** Knit every row, inc one st each side every 4 rows 15 times: 56 sts.

Knit even until sleeve measures 17 (17, 18)" from CO edge. BO all sts.

FINISHING

With crochet hook, and right side facing starting at right front bottom corner, work one round of single crochet around right front, hood edge, left front and bottom edge of jacket. Fasten off.

Sew zipper in place.

Using a smooth matching color yarn, sew sleeve seams, then sew sleeves in place.

Do not block jacket.

FAUX FUR JACKET

Designed by Jean Leinhauser

Elegance personified! Slip into this frankly faux jacket for an elegant evening event. You'll be the belle of the party!

FAUX FUR JACKET

SIZES	Small	Medium	Large	X- Large
Body Bust Measurements	34"	36"	38"	40"- 42"
Finished Bust Measurements	37"	40"	42 1/2"	45 3/4"

Note: Instructions are written for size Small; changes for sizes Medium, Large and X-Large are in parentheses.

Materials

Faux fur type yarn
 15 3/4 (15 3/4, 17 1/2, 17 1/2) oz black
Sport weight yarn
 10 (10, 10, 15) oz black
Note: Photographed model made with Lion Brand® Fun Fur #153 Black and Lion Brand® Baby Soft® #153 Black
2 stitch holders
Size 11 (8 mm) knitting needles
 (or size required for gauge)

Gauge

14 sts = 4" with one stand of each yarn held tog

Stitch Guide

M1 (make 1): Make one st by picking up horizontal bar lying before next stitch and knitting into back of this bar: increase made.

INSTRUCTIONS

Note: Entire garment is worked with two strands (one strand of each yarn) held tog.

BACK

With 2 strands of yarn (one strand of each yarn held tog), CO 61 (66, 71, 76) sts.

Knit each row until piece measures about 5 3/4 (6, 6 1/4, 6 1/2)" from CO row.

Increase Row: Inc one st at each end of row.

Work even for 5", then rep Increase Row once more: 65 (70, 75, 80) sts. Work even until piece measures 11 1/2 (11 1/2, 12, 12)" from CO row.

SHAPE ARMHOLES

BO 3 sts at beg of next 2 rows, then 2 sts at beg of next 2 rows: 55 (60, 65, 70) sts. Dec one st at each end on next row, then every row 3 (3, 3, 4) times more: 47 (52, 57, 60) sts. Work even until armhole measures 8 (8 1/2, 9, 9 1/2)", ending by working a wrong-side row.

SHAPE NECK AND SHOULDER

For sizes small, medium and large only:

BO 7 (8, 9) sts at beg of next 4 rows. BO rem 19 (20, 21) sts for back of neck.

For size X-Large only:

BO 9 sts at beg of next 2 rows, then 10 sts at beg of next 2 rows. BO rem 22 sts for back of neck.

LEFT FRONT

With 2 strands of yarn, CO 32 (36, 39, 42) sts.

Knit each row until piece measures 5 3/4 (6, 6 1/4, 6 1/2)" from CO row.

Increase Row: Inc one st at side edge of next row.

Work even in garter st for 5", then inc one st at side edge: 34 (38, 41, 44) sts.

Work even until piece measures 11 1/2 (11 1/2, 12, 12)" from CO row, ending by working a wrong-side row.

SHAPE ARMHOLE

Row 1 (right side): BO 3 sts at beg of row, knit across.

Row 2 (wrong side): Work even.

Row 3: BO 2 sts at beg of row, knit across: 29 (33, 36, 39) sts.

Row 4: Work even.

Dec one st at beg of next row, then one st at same edge every other row 3 (3, 3, 4) times more: 25 (29, 32, 34) sts.

Work even until armhole measures 6 (6 1/2, 7, 7 1/2)", ending with a wong-side row.

SHAPE NECK AND SHOULDER

Row 1 (right side): Knit to last 7 (9, 10, 11) sts and place them on a holder for collar: 18 (20, 22, 23) sts.

Row 2 (wrong side): K2tog, knit across.

Row 3: Knit.

Rep Rows 2 and 3, three times more: 14 (16, 18, 19) sts. Work until armhole measures same as back, ending with a wrong-side row.

SHAPE SHOULDER

For Sizes Small, Medium and Large only:
Row 1 (right side): BO 7 (8, 9) sts, knit across.

Row 2 (wrong side): Knit

BO rem 7 (8, 9) sts.

For Size X-Large only:
Row 1 (right side): BO 9 sts, knit across.

Row 2 (wrong side): Knit.

Row 3: BO rem 10 sts.

RIGHT FRONT

Work same as Left Front, reversing shaping.

SLEEVE (Make 2)

With 2 strands of yarn held tog, CO 26 (28, 30, 34) sts. Knit 5 rows.

Increase Row: K1, M1, knit to last st, M1, K1.

Knit each row, repeating Increase Row every 6 rows 9 times more: 46 (48, 50, 54) sts.

Work even until piece measures 16 1/2 (17, 17, 17)" from beg or desired length to underarm, ending with a wrong-side row.

SHAPE CAP

BO 3 sts at beg of next 2 rows: 40 (42, 44, 48) sts.

Decrease Row: Dec one st at each end of next row, then every other row 7 times more. BO rem 24 (26, 28, 32) sts.

FINISHING

Sew shoulder seams.

COLLAR

With RS facing and 2 strands of yarn held tog, K7 (9, 10, 11) sts from right front holder, pick up and K32 (33, 34, 35) sts evenly around neck edge, K7 (9, 10, 11) sts from left front holder: 46 (51, 54, 57) sts. Knit 10 rows. BO tightly.

Sew sleeves into armholes; sew side and sleeve seams.

CUTE CARDI

Designed by Jodi Lewanda

Buttons and bows decorate this darling sweater made especially for a cherished child.
She knows that she's just too cute!

CUTE CARDI

SIZES	2	4
Body Chest Measurements	21"	23"
Finished Chest Measurements	27"	29"

Note: Instructions are written for size 2; changes for size 4 are in parentheses.

Materials

Bulky weight yarn
14 (16) oz multi color
4 (4) 1" buttons
Note: Photographed model made with Lion Brand® Landscapes, #276 Summer Fields and JHB International buttons #49804.
Stitch markers
Size 10 (6 mm) knitting needles (or size required for gauge)

Gauge

12 sts = 4"

Stitch Guide:

To make front body buttonholes:

With right side facing, K2, BO 2, knit across row.

Next row: Knit across row to BO sts, turn, CO 2 sts, turn, K2.

INSTRUCTIONS

BACK

Waistband

CO 6 (8) sts.

Knit every row until piece measures 21 1/2" (22 1/2") from CO edge. BO all sts.

Body

Measure 6" (6") in from each end along long side of waistband and place marker.

CO 6 sts, pick up and knit 28 (32) sts from waistband between markers, CO 6 sts: 40 (44) sts.

Knit in garter st until piece measures 14" (15") from beginning (including waistband), ending by working a right-side row. BO 14 (15) sts, knit across center 12 (14) sts and place on a holder, BO last 14 (15) sts.

LEFT FRONT

Waistband

CO 6 (8) sts.

Knit every row until piece measures 11 3/4" (12 1/4") from CO edge. BO all sts.

Body

Measure 6" (6") in from one end along long side of waistband and place marker.

CO 6 sts, then with marked end of waistband to the right, pick up and knit 16 (19) sts from marker to end of waistband: 22 (25) sts. Knit until piece measures 2 1/2" (2 1/2") less than back, ending by working a right-side row.

Shape neck

BO 6 (7) sts at neck edge, knit across: 16 (18) sts.

BO one st at neck edge every other row 2 (3) times: 14 (15) sts.

Work even until piece measure same as back. BO all sts.

Place 4 (4) markers (for buttons) evenly spaced, along front edge, starting at center of waistband and ending 1/2" (3/4") below neck edge BO.

RIGHT FRONT

Waistband

CO 6 (8) sts.

Knit every row until piece measures 11 1/4" (11 3/4") from CO edge, ending by working a wrong-side row.

Place a buttonhole as follows:

Row 1: K2 (3), BO next 2 sts, K2 (3).

Row 2: K2 (3), turn CO 2 sts, turn K2 (3).

Knit until piece measures 11 3/4" (12 1/4") from CO edge. BO all sts.

Body

Measure 6" (6") in from one end along long side of waistband (non-buttonhole end) and place marker.

With right side facing (buttonhole is at right edge), pick up and knit 16 (19) sts from buttonhole end of waistband to marker, CO 6 sts: 22 (25) sts.

Knit, placing buttonholes along front edge to match left front button markers.

When piece measures 2 1/2" (2 1/2") less than back and ending by working a right-side row, shape neck:

Shape neck

Next row: Knit across row until 6 (7) sts rem at neck edge. BO 6 (7) sts.

Cut yarn and reattach at beginning of BO to complete shaping. BO one st every other row at neck edge 2 (3) times: 14 (15) sts.

Continue to knit until piece measure same as back. BO all sts.

SLEEVES (Make 2)

Starting at bottom, CO 20 (22) sts.

Knit every row, inc one st each side every 10 rows 6 (6) times: 32 (34) sts. Knit even until sleeve measures 10" (11") from CO edge. BO all sts.

FINISHING

Sew shoulder seams.

Neck

With right side facing, starting at right front neck edge corner, pick up and knit 6 (7) sts along right front BO edge, 8 (8) sts along right front, 12 (14) sts from back st holder, 8 (8) sts from left front and 6 (7) sts along left front BO edge: 40 (44) sts

Knit 2 rows. BO all sts.

Sew sleeves in place, centering at shoulder seam. Sew underarm and side seams. Sew buttons to left front at markers.

Weave in all ends.

Tie tabs of front and back waistbands into bow.

VEST OF MANY COLORS

Designed by Valentina Devine

Choose many colors and change them at random for the beautiful abstract effect in this vest. Then be prepared to see the approving glances as you twirl.

VEST OF MANY COLORS

SIZES	Small	Medium	Large
Body Bust Measurements	30"- 34"	36"- 40"	42"- 46"
Finished Bust Measurements	40"	44"	48"

Note: Instructions are written for size Small; changes for sizes Medium and Large are in parentheses.

Materials

Worsted weight yarn
  24 (28, 32) oz total of a variety of colors
Note: Photographed model made with Prism™ Yarns Quadro Autumn
Pearl Cotton Embroidery Thread (optional)
Size 10 (6 mm) knitting needles (or size required for gauge)

Gauge

22 sts = 4"

Notes:

This garment is knit in individual strips and worked on the diagonal; therefore when the strips are sewn together the appearance is a somewhat abstract chevron look.

The knitter has the choice of using various colors and changing them at random; as Kaffe Fassett would say: "When in doubt, reach for a new color."

INSTRUCTIONS

A: LONGER STRIPS (Make 4 strips for back, 2 strips for each front)

CO 2 sts.

Row 1: Knit 2 sts.

Row 2: Increase one stitch at beginning of row, work even to end of row.

Rep Row 2 until there are 21 (25, 29) sts. The row should measure approximately 4 (4 1/2 , 5)" across.

Increase /Decrease Rows

Row 1: Increase one st at beginning of row, work even

to end of row.

Row 2: Decrease one st at beginning of row, work even to end of row.

Rep Rows 1 and 2, increasing on one side of the strip and decreasing one st on the other side of the strip until longer side of strip is 35 1/2 (36, 36 1/2)" long.

Last Row: Decrease one st at beginning of row and one st at end of row.

Rep Last Row until 3 sts remain. K3 tog. Cut yarn.

B: UNDERARM STRIPS (Make 2 shorter strips)

CO 2 sts.

Row 1: Knit 2 sts.

Row 2: Increase one stitch at beginning of row, work even to end of row.

Rep Row 2 until there are 21 (25, 29) sts. The row should measure approximately 4 (41/2, 5)" across.

VEST OF MANY COLORS

Increase /Decrease Rows

Row 1: Increase one st at beginning of row, work even to end of row.

Row 2: Decrease one st at beginning of row, work even to end of row.

Rep Rows 1 and 2 increasing on one side of the strip and decreasing one st on the other side of the strip until longer side of strip is 29" or desired length.

Last Row: Decrease one st at beginning of row and decrease one st at end of row.

Rep Last Row until 3 sts remain. K3 tog. Strip should measure approximately 29" long.

C: CENTER FRONT STRIPS WITH V-NECK (make 2 shorter strips)

CO 2 sts and work same as Longer Strips until piece measures 32". BO all sts on needle (rather than decreasing on both sides) resulting in the perfect V-neck.

NECK TIE

CO 10 sts. Knit until piece measures 60". BO all sts.

FINISHING

Using pearl cotton embroidery, whip stitch the vest strips together following the diagram making a practically invisible seam. Centering the neck tie and back of neck, whipstitch neck tie in place along right front, back and left front neck edges. Fold portion of neck tie sewn to neck in half horizontally and tack in place forming a rolled neck. Leave remaining portion of neck tie on left and right fronts free and unfolded. If desired, knot each end of neck tie.

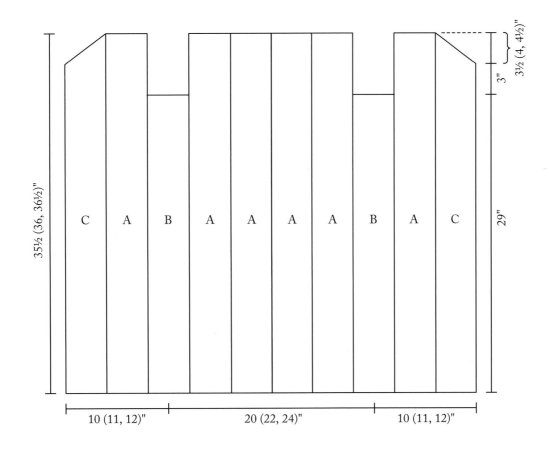

DIAGONAL BLOCKS TOPPER

Designed by Nazanin S. Fard

The subtle combination of red and grey set off the interesting diagonal blocks on this easy-to-wear jacket. Sure to win nods of approval wherever it's worn.

DIAGONAL BLOCKS TOPPER

SIZES	Small	Medium	Large
Body Bust Measurements	36"	40"	44"
Finished Bust Measurements	40"	44"	48"

Note: *Instructions are written for size Small; changes for sizes Medium and Large are in parentheses.*

Materials

Sport weight yarn

14 (20, 28) oz gray (A)

14 (20, 28) oz red (B)

Note: *Photographed model made with Patons® Kroy #54046 Flagstone (A) and #54727 Retro Red (B) and buttons by Favorite Findings*

2 stitch holders or waste yarn

Six 1/2" ladybug buttons

Size 6 (4 mm) straight knitting needles (or size required for gauge)

40" Size 6 (4 mm) circular knitting needle

GAUGE

20 sts = 4" with two strands of yarn

Stitch Guide

M1: Insert needle under the yarn between the stitch just made and the next stitch and twist it. Knit in the twisted yarn loop.

SSK: Slip next 2 stitches as if to knit, move them back to left needle, knit both together through the back loops.

K2tog: Knit next 2 stitches tog.

One-row buttonhole: Knit or sl 2 sts onto right needle and sl 2nd st over first, knit or sl another st to right needle and sl 2nd st over first (2 sts BO), sl rem st on left needle back to left needle and CO on 2 sts, knit across sts.

INSTRUCTIONS

FULL BLOCK (Make 6):

With straight needles and two strands of A, CO 3 sts.

Row 1: Knit.

Row 2: K1, knit in front then back and front of same st, K1: 5 sts.

Row 3: With B, knit.

Row 4: With A, K1, (M1, K1) twice: 7 sts.

Row 5: With A, knit.

Row 6: With A, K1, M1, knit until there is one stitch left on needle, M1, K1: 9 sts

Repeat rows 5 and 6 alternating colors every other row and until you have 65 (73, 81) sts at the end of row 62 (70, 78).

Row 63 (71, 79): With A, knit.

Row 64 (72, 80): With A, K1, SSK, knit until 3 sts remain on needle, K2tog, K1: 63 (71, 79) sts.

Repeat rows 63 and 64 alternating colors every other row and until you have 3 sts at the end of row 126 (134, 142).

BO all sts.

PARTIAL BLOCK (Make 2):

Work same as full block through Row 62 (70, 78), then working decreases continue until there are 43 sts on the needle. Place all sts on holder or waste yarn.

SLEEVES (Make 2):

With straight needles and two strands of A, CO 42, (46, 50) sts.

DIAGONAL BLOCKS TOPPER

Work in Garter St for 5 ridges (10 rows).

Begin alternating colors A and B and increasing 1 st both ends every 4th row 14 times, then every 8 rows 5 times, and every 12 rows 5 times: 90 (94, 98) sts. Work even until sleeve measures 17½" (17½", 18"). BO all sts.

FINISHING:

Sew blocks together as shown in the diagram, leaving front opening. Sew sleeves to the body. Sew underarm and sleeve seams.

Bottom band:

From bottom edge, with circular needle and two strands of A, pick up 140 (148, 156) sts. Do not join. Work in Garter St for 6 ridges (12 rows). BO all sts.

Front and neck band:

With right side facing, using circular needle and two strands of A, starting from right front edge, pick up 320 (330, 340) sts around both fronts and back neck as follows:

Pick up 88 (91, 94) sts from right front, knit 43 sts from holder, pick up 58 (62, 66) sts from back neck, knit 43 sts from holder, then pick up 88 (91, 94) sts from left front.

Rows 1 through 5: Knit.

Row 6 (right side: buttonhole row): At the right front, K3, *one-row buttonhole, k15 (13, 13); repeat from * until 6 buttonholes have been made. Knit to end of row as established.

Rows 7 through 11: Knit.

BO all sts loosely.

Block jacket to size.

Sew buttons across from buttonholes.

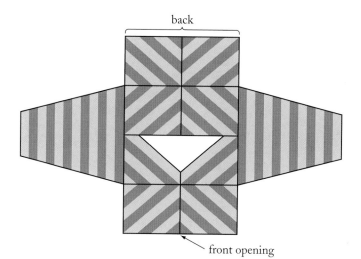

front opening

YES, IT'S GARTER STITCH

Designed by Rita Weiss

Using only the knit stitch, red and white yarns combine to create a houndstooth effect in this great hat and scarf set.

YES, IT'S GARTER STITCH

Size
Scarf: Approximately 10 1/2" x 54"
Hat: Fits up to 22" head

Materials
Medium weight yarn
  5 oz red (A)
  5 oz white (B)
Note: Photographed model made with Red Heart® Super Saver® #332 Ranch Red (A) and #311White
Size 7 (4.5 mm) knitting needles
  (or size required for gauge)

Gauge
10 sts = 3" in garter st

Stitch Guide
K1B: Knit 1 st in row below.

SCARF

INSTRUCTIONS
With A, CO 35 sts.

Row 1: With A, knit.

Row 2: With A, knit. Attach B.

Row 3 (right side): With B, K3, *K1B, K1; rep from * to last 2 sts, K2.

Row 4 (wrong side): With B, knit.

Row 5: With A, K2, K1B, *K1, K1B; rep from * to last 2 sts, K2.

Row 6: With A, knit.

Rep Rows 3 through 6 until piece measures 54" from CO row, ending by working Row 6. Knit one row. BO. Weave in all ends.

HAT

INSTRUCTIONS

With A, CO 62 sts.

Rows 1 and 2: With A, knit.

Row 3 (right side): With A, *K1, K1B; rep from * to last 2 sts, K2.

Row 4 (wrong side): With A, knit. Attach B.

Row 5: With B, K2, *K1B, K1; rep from * across.

Row 6: With B, knit.

Rep Rows 3 through 6 until piece measures 6" from CO row, ending with Row 6. Cut B.

SHAPE CROWN

Note: Work with A only for crown.

Rows 1, 2 and 3: Knit.

Row 4: K3, *K6, K2tog; rep from * to last 3 sts, K3: 55 sts.

Row 5 and all odd rows: Knit.

Row 6: K3, *K5, K2tog; rep from * to last 3 sts, K3: 48 sts.

Row 8: *K4, K2tog; rep from * across: 40 sts.

Row 10: *K3, K2tog; rep from * across: 32 sts.

Row 12: *K2, K2tog; rep from * across: 24 sts.

Row 14: *K1, K2tog; rep from * across: 16 sts.

Row 15: Knit.

Cut yarn, leaving a long tail. Weave yarn through rem 16 sts and pull up tightly to secure. Join back seam. Weave in all yarn ends.

MIGHTY MITERS

Designed by Donna Druchunas

Easy to make with just eight mitered squares, this wearable jacket is accented with basic black sleeves and trim.

MIGHTY MITERS

SIZES	Small	Medium	Large
Body Bust Measurements	30"- 34"	36"- 40"	42"- 46"
Finished Bust Measurements	41"	45"	49"

Note: Instructions are written for size Small; changes for sizes Medium and Large are in parentheses.

Materials

Bulky weight wool or wool-blend yarn,
   400 (600, 700) grams black
   600 (700, 800) grams variegated

Note: Photographed model made with Plymouth Yarn® Encore Chunky #217 Black and #7127 Variegated.

One 22" separating zipper

Size 9 (5.5 mm) and 10 1/2 (6.5 mm) knitting needles
   (or size required for gauge)

Gauge

14 sts = 4" with larger needles

Stitch Guide

P2SSO (pass 2 sts over knit st): Sl 2 sts one at a time to right needle, K1; then pass these 2 sl sts tog over knit st: P2SSO made,

INSTRUCTIONS

MITERED SQUARES (Make 8)

With larger needles and variegated yarn, CO 71 (85, 99) sts.

Knit 1 row (WS).

Work double-dec patt:

Row 1 (RS): K34 (41, 48) st, sl 2, K1, P2SSO, K34 (41, 48): 69 (83, 97) sts.

Row 2 and all odd (wrong side) rows: Knit all sts.

Row 3: K33 (40, 47), sl 2, K1, P2SSO, K33 (40, 47): 67 (81, 95) sts.

Row 5: K32 (39, 46), sl 2, K1, P2SSO, k32 (39, 46): 65 (79, 93) sts.

Row 7: K31 (38, 45), sl 2, K1, P2SSO, K31 (38, 45): 63 (77, 91) sts.

Continue knitting, working one st fewer before and after the center (sl 2, k1, P2SSO) on each right-side row until one st rem. Fasten off.

SLEEVES (Make 2)

Starting at bottom with smaller needles and solid yarn, CO 28 (30, 32) sts.

Knit for 2". Change to larger needles.

Continue knitting and inc one st each side next row and every 5 rows 9 (11, 11) times, then every 6 rows 8 (9, 10) times: 66 (70, 74) sts.

Continue even until sleeve measures 18" (19", 20)" from CO edge. BO all sts.

FINISHING

Sew four squares together for back following photograph for orientation of squares.

Sew two squares together for each front.

Seam shoulders, leaving approx 4" open on each side of center for neck.

Sew in sleeves. Sew underarm and side seams.

Bottom Band

With solid yarn, smaller needles and right side facing, pick up and knit 140 (168, 196) sts across bottom edge of sweater. Knit 20 rows. BO all sts.

Right Front Band

With solid yarn, smaller needles and right side facing,

pick up and knit 70 (84, 98) sts along right front edge of sweater. Knit 4 rows. BO all sts.

Left Front Band

Work as for right front.

Neckband

With solid yarn, smaller needles and right side facing, pick up and knit 4 sts in front band, one st in each st to shoulder seam, place marker, one st in each st across back to shoulder seam, place marker, one st in each st to front band, then 4 sts in front band.

Note: *Number of sts will vary based on size and exact measurement of neck opening.*

Row 1: Knit.

Row 2: *Knit to 2 sts before shoulder seam marker, K2tog, sl marker, K2tog, rep from * once, knit to end of row.

Knit 2 rows even.

BO all sts.

Weave in ends.

Sew in zipper.

PRETTY PETITE PONCHO

Designed by Rebecca Hatcher

Not quite a cape, too big for a collar, this petite poncho can add a wonderful spark of color and makes the perfect addition to anyone's drab wardrobe.

PRETTY PETITE PONCHO

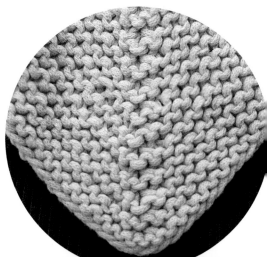

SIZES	Small	Medium	Large
Body Bust Measurements	32"-34"	36"-38"	40"-42"
Finished Garment Lower Circumference	76"	84"	92"
Finished Garment Length	13"	15"	17"

Note: *Instructions are written for size Small; changes for sizes Medium and Large are in parentheses.*

Materials

Bulky cotton yarn,
  375 (500, 625) yds
Note: *Photographed model made with Rowan Cotton Tape, #544 Bamboo.*
Stitch marker
2 Stitch holders
36" Size 11 (5 mm) circular knitting needle
  (or size required for gauge)
Spare Size 11 straight needle

Gauge

12 sts = 4"

Stitch Guide

M1 (make 1): Make one st by picking up horizontal bar lying before next stitch and knitting into back of this bar: increase made.

SSK: Slip next 2 sts as it to knit, move them back to left needle, knit both together through back loops.

INSTRUCTIONS

Note: *Do not join new yarn at the edge of the work, since this will be the edge of the garment.*

Starting at lower edge, CO 120 (132, 144) sts. Do not join; work back and forth in rows.

Set up row (wrong side): K60 (66, 72), place marker, K60 (66, 72).

Set up row (wrong side): K42 (48, 54) and place on a stitch holder for right back, BO 36 sts, knit to end of row for left back.

Work only on last 42 (48, 54) sts for left back as follows:

Row 1 (right side) (RS): K1, M1, K38 (44, 50), SSK, K1: 42 (48, 54) sts.

Row 2 (wrong side): Knit.

Rep these 2 rows until piece measures approximately 13 1/2 (15 3/4, 18)" from CO edge on front, ending on a wrong-side row. Cut yarn, and place these sts on a stitch holder.

RIGHT BACK

Rejoin yarn at neck edge and work right back sts as follows:

Row 1 (right side): K1, K2tog, K38 (44, 50), M1, K1.

Row 2 (wrong side): Knit.

Rep these 2 rows until piece measures approximately 13 1/2 (15 3/4, 18)" from CO edge, ending with a wrong-side row.

Transfer sts from stitch holder to spare needle, so that point of needle is at neck edge. Using live yarn from right back, and with right-side facing, join left and right backs using 3-needle technique (see page 126).

Weave in all ends.

FRONT

Row 1 (right side): K1, M1, K57 (63, 69), SSK, sl marker, K2tog, K57 (63, 69), M1, K1: 120 (132, 144) sts. **Note:** *The incs and decs are worked in pairs throughout, so that the overall st count does not change.*

Row 2 (wrong side): Knit.

Rep Rows 1 and 2 until piece measures approximately 9 (10 1/2, 12)" from CO edge, ending with a right-side row. Continue working on left back.

LEFT BACK

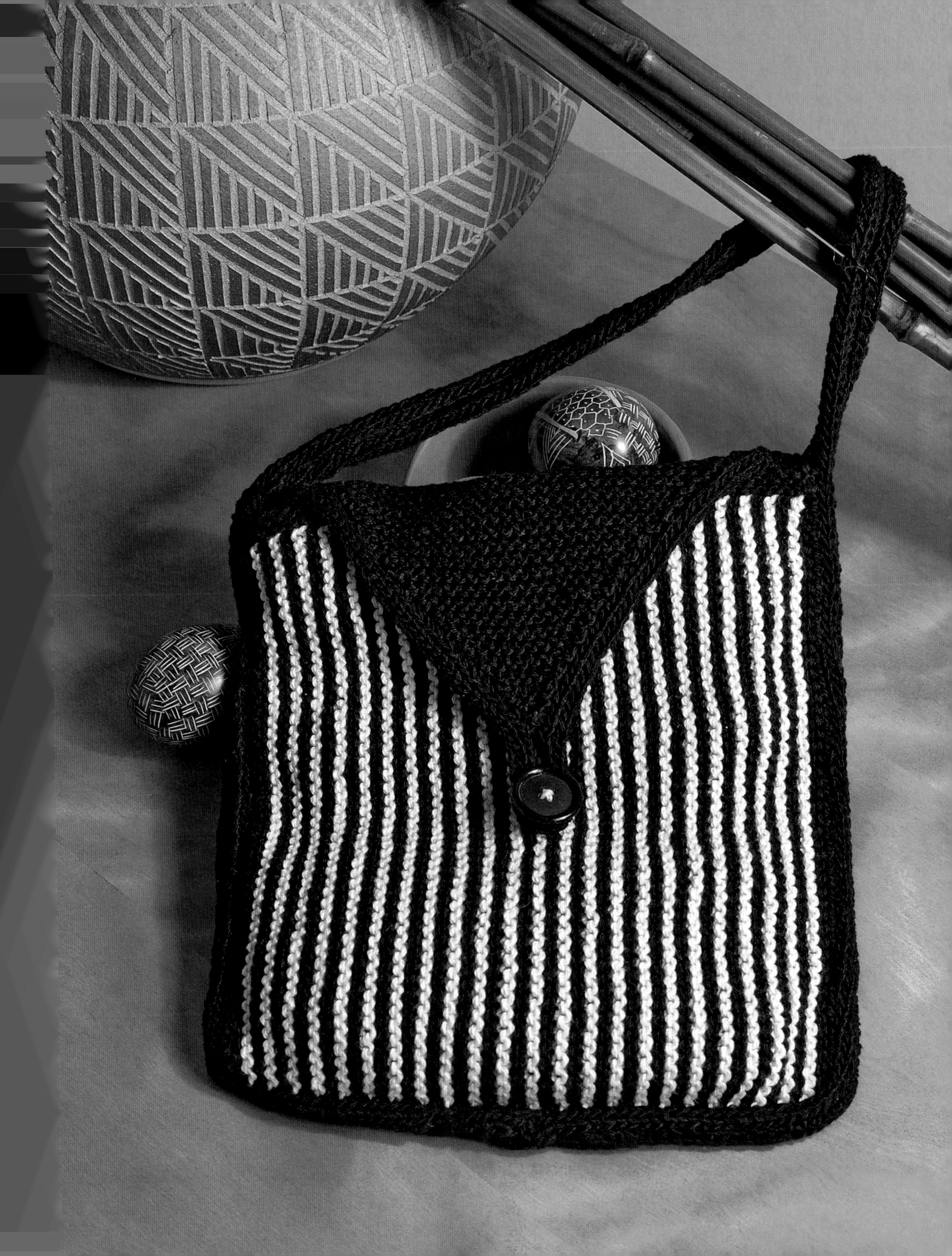

STRIPES ON THE GO

Designed by Jodi Lewanda

Dramatic black and white stripes set off this easy-to-make tote and accessory set. Carry them together, or let each piece shine on its own.

STRIPES ON THE GO

Size:
Tote: 10 1/4" wide x 11 1/4" long (plus handle)
Accessory case: 3 1/2" wide x 6" long (plus handle)

Materials
Worsted weight cotton or cotton blend yarn
5 1/2 oz main color (MC)
3 1/2 oz contrast color (CC)
*Note: Photographed model was made with JCA Reynolds
    Saucy, #899 Black (MC) and #817 Ecru (CC)*
1 large (1 1/4") button for tote
1 medium (3/4") button for accessory case
Stitch markers
Size 6 (4 mm) knitting needles (or size required
    for gauge)
Size 6 (4 mm) double-pointed needles for I-cord

Gauge
20 sts = 4" in garter st with size 6 needles

Stitch Guide
To make I-cord: Using one double-pointed needle and
MC, CO 4 sts.

Row 1: With another double-pointed needle, knit 4; do
not turn.

Slide sts to opposite end of the needle.

Row 2: Take yarn around the back side of sts and with
second needle, knit 4; do not turn.

Slide sts to opposite end of needle.

Repeat Rows 1 and 2 until cord is desired length. BO.

TOTE

INSTRUCTIONS
With MC, CO 100 sts.

Row 1 (wrong side): Knit.

Rows 2 and 3: With CC, knit 2 rows.

Rows 4 and 5: With MC, knit 2 rows.

Repeat rows 2 through 5 until piece measures about
9 1/2", ending with 2 MC rows.

With CC, knit 2 rows.

With MC, knit 1 row.

With MC, BO.

TOTE FRONT TRIM
Measure in 1/2" from corners along one short side and
place markers.

With right side facing and MC, pick up and knit 47 sts
between markers.

Knit 3 rows.

BO.

TOTE FLAP
Measure in 1/2" from corners along opposite short side
and place markers.

With right side facing and MC, pick up and knit 47 sts
between markers.

Knit 3 rows.

BO 3 sts at beg of next 2 rows: 41 sts.

Next row: Dec 1 st at each end as follows: K2tog tbl,
knit across row until 2 sts rem, K2tog.

Next row: Knit across.

Repeat last 2 rows until 3 sts rem.

Knit 1 row.

BO.

I-CORDS

With MC, make one 16" I-cord (for flap and button loop).

With MC, make one 88" I-cord (for tote edge plus 19" handle — lengthen or shorten as desired).

FINISHING

Attach 16" I-cord to tote flap as follows: Pin cord to flap, with each end at an upper corner and mid cord at flap point, forming a button loop. Stitch I-cord in place.

Attach 88" I-cord to tote as follows: Fold tote in half. Pin cord to tote, with cord ends meeting at center bottom of tote, encircling tote twice forming double I-cord edge along tote sides and bottom and forming double I-cord handle. Stitch I-cords to tote and to each other, forming 'sides' of tote and trimming bottom edge. Stitch handle I-cords together.

Sew button to front of tote. Weave in ends.

ACCESSORY CASE

INSTRUCTIONS

With MC, CO 14 sts.

Row 1 and 2: With MC, knit 2 rows.

Row 3 and 4: With CC, knit 2 rows.

Repeat rows 1 through 4 until piece measures 11 3/4".

With MC, knit 4 rows.

ACCESSORY CASE FLAP

Next row: Dec 1 st at each end as follows: K2tog tbl, knit across row until 2 sts rem, K2tog.

Next row: Knit across.

Repeat last 2 rows until 2 sts rem.

Knit 1 row.

BO.

I-CORDS

With MC, make one 6" I-cord (for flap and button loop).

With MC, make one 19" I-cord (for case edge plus 6" handle; add or shorten as desired).

FINISHING

Attach 6" I-cord to accessory case flap as follows: Pin cord to flap, with each end at an upper corner and mid cord at flap point, forming a button loop. Stitch I-cord in place.

Attach 19" I-cord to accessory case as follows: Fold case in half. Pin cord to case, with cord ends meeting at center bottom of case, and forming handle. Stitch I-cord to each side of case, forming 'sides' of case and trimming bottom edge.

Sew button to front of case. Weave in ends.

DIAMONDS ARE A GIRL'S BEST FRIEND

*Designed by
Nazanin S. Fard*

*The lacy diamonds in this
beautiful shawl are sure to
sparkle and shine as they
go from day to night as an
elegant accessory.*

DIAMONDS ARE A GIRL'S BEST FRIEND

Size

Finished Size: Approx. 82" x 50" x 50"

Materials

Sport weight cotton yarn

14 oz lilac

Note: *Photographed model made with Patons® Grace #246060 French Lilac*

Size 6 (4 mm) knitting needles (or size required for gauge)

Gauge

20 sts = 4"

Stitch Guide

Sl 1K: Slip the first stitch with yarn in back.

Sl 1P: Slip the first stitch with yarn in front.

PU 1: Pick up and knit 1 stitch.

PS 1: Pass the previously picked up stitch over the last stitch on right needle.

Inc: Increase by knitting in front and back of the next stitch.

INSTRUCTIONS

SHAWL

CO 3 sts.

Row 1 and every odd-numbered rows: Knit.

Row 2: K1, K3 in next st, K1: 5 sts.

Row 4: K2, YO, K1, YO, K2: 7 sts..

Row 6: K2, YO, K3, YO, K2: 9 sts.

Row 8: K2, YO, K5, YO, K2: 11 sts.

Row 10: K2, YO, K7, YO, K2: 13 sts.

Row 12: K2, YO, K4, YO, SSK, K3, YO, K2: 15 sts.

Row 14: K2, YO, *K1, YO, SSK, K5, K2tog, YO, rep from * until 3 sts rem on needle, K1, YO, K2: 2 sts inc.

Row 16: K2, YO, *K3, YO, SSK, K3, K2tog, YO, rep from * until there are 5 stitches left on needle, K3, YO, K2.

Row 18: K2, YO, *K5, YO, SSK, K1, K2tog, YO, rep from * until 7 sts rem on needle, K5, YO, K2.

Row 20: K2, YO, *K7, YO, K3tog, YO, rep from * until 9 sts rem on needle, K7, YO, K2.

Row 22: K2, YO, *K4, YO, SSK, K2, k2tog, YO, rep from * until 11 sts rem on needle, K4, YO, SSK, K3, YO, k2.

Repeat rows 14 through 23 until desired length.

BO all sts loosely. Do not cut yarn.

BORDER:

CO 2 sts.

Row 1: Sl 1K, K1.

Row 2: Sl 1P, K1, PU 1.

Row 3: Sl 1K, inc, K1: 4 sts.

Row 4: Sl 1P, K3, PU 1, PS 1.

Row 5: Sl 1K, K1, inc, K1: 5 sts.

Row 6: Sl 1P, K4, PU 1, PS 1.

Row 7: Sl 1K, K2, inc, K1: 6 sts.

Row 8: Sl 1P, K5, PU 1, PS 1.

Row 9: Sl 1K, K3, inc, K1: 7 sts.

Row 10: Sl 1P, K6, PU 1, PS 1.

Row 11: Sl 1K, K4, inc, K1: 8 sts.

Row 12: Sl 1P, K7, PU 1, PS 1.

Row 13: Sl 1K, K5, inc, K1: 9 sts.

Row 14: Sl 1P, K8, PU 1, PS 1.

Row 15: Sl 1K, K5, K2tog, K1: 8 sts.

Row 16: Sl 1P, K7, PU 1, PS 1.

Row 17: Sl 1K, K4, K2tog, K1: 7 sts.

Row 18: Sl 1P, K6, PU 1, PS 1.

Row 19: Sl 1K, K3, K2tog, K1: 6 sts.

Row 20: Sl 1P, K5, PU 1, PS 1.

Row 21: Sl 1K, K2, k2tog, K1: 5 sts.

Row 22: Sl 1P, K4, PU 1, PS 1.

Row 23: Sl 1K, K1, K2tog, K1: 4 sts.

Row 24: Sl 1P, K3, PU 1, PS 1.

Row 25: Sl 1K, K2tog, K1: 3 sts.

Row 26: Sl 1P, K2, PU 1, PS 1.

Row 27: Sl 1K, K2tog: 2 sts.

Row 28: Sl 1P, K1, PU 1, PS 1.

Repeat rows 1 through 28 for patt, working border along two shorter (side) edges of shawl triangle.

FINISHING:

Block shawl to size.

TRIANGLE PATCHWORK

Designed by Joyce Renee Wyatt

A most innovative project, the jacket is made with 86 triangles that are joined, following a chart, to create a striking garment.

TRIANGLE PATCHWORK

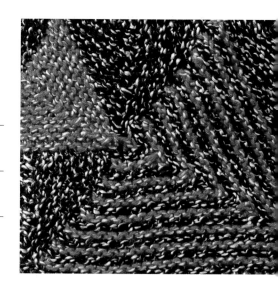

SIZES	Small	Medium	Large	X-Large
Body Bust Measurements	32"-34"	36"-38"	40"-44"	46"-42"
Finished Bust Measurements	37"	41"	46 1/4"	51 3/4"

Note: Instructions are written for size Small; changes for sizes Medium, Large and X-Large are in parentheses.

Materials

Worsted weight acrylic/nylon blend yarn
  12 (18, 14, 30) oz burgundy
  18 (24, 30, 30) oz black
Note: Photographed model made with Red Heart® Fiesta® #6915 Burgundy (A) and #6012 Black (B)
Seven 3/4" buttons
Tapestry needle
Stitch markers
Stitch holder
24" Size 7 (4.5 mm) circular needles for trim
24" Size 10 (6 mm) circular needles
Note: Because of the large number of stitches that are on the needle at the same time circular needles are recommended. Do not join; knit back and forth in rows.

Gauge

18 sts and 36 rows = 4" with smaller needles
16 sts and 32 rows = 4" with larger needles

Stitch Guide

DD (Double Decrease): Slip 1 st as to knit, K2tog, pass the slip st over.

SSK (slip, slip, knit): Slip next 2 sts as to knit, one at a time, to right needle; insert left needle into front of these 2 sts from right to left and then knit them tog.

PU: Pick up stitches

Wyib: With yarn in back

Wyif: With yarn in front

INSTRUCTIONS

This jacket is constructed of triangles that are joined together as they are added in rows.

TRIANGLE FOUNDATION

Basic Triangle:
Side AC equals Side BC plus 1 extra stitch.
(16 + 16 + 1 = 33 sts), (18 + 18 + 1 = 37 sts),
(19 + 19 + 1 = 39 sts), (21 + 21 + 1 = 43 sts).

Small Triangle Construction Methods

Method 1: CO 17 (19, 20, 22) sts and PU 16 (18, 19, 21) sts **or,**

Method 2: PU 16 (18, 19, 21) sts and CO 17 (19, 20, 22) sts **or,**

Method 3: PU 33 (37, 39, 43) sts.

A — B
Small Triangle #1
16 sts — 16 sts
C + 1 st

Note: Long arrow = direction of the DD.

JACKET

Follow chart on page 57 for placement of units and work colors to correspond to photograph. Start at lower edge of center back with Triangle #1 working Row 1 as follows with larger circular needle: With A, CO 33 (37, 39, 43) sts.

Rows 1, 4, 7, 10, 13: Knit across.

Row 2: K1, SSK, K12 (14, 15, 17), DD, K12 (14, 15, 17), K2tog, K1: 29 (33, 35, 39) sts.

56

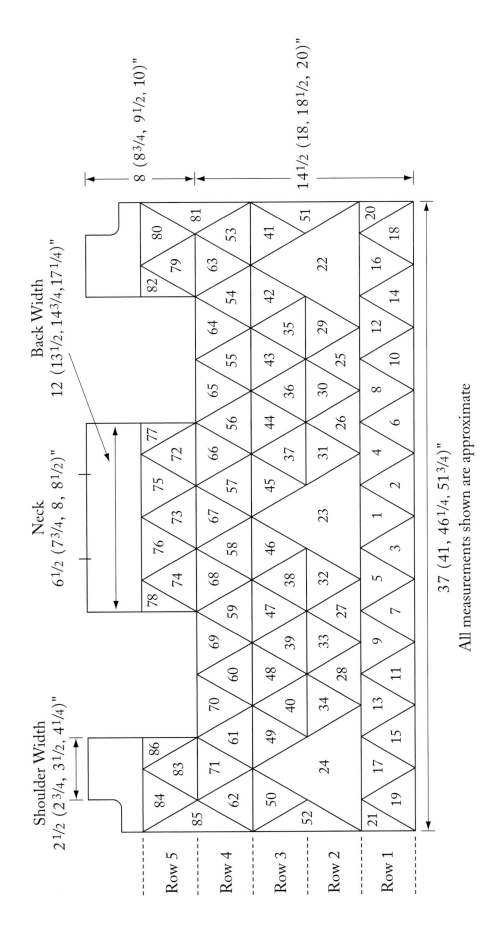

TRIANGLE PATCHWORK

Row 3: K13 (15, 16, 18), DD, K13 (15, 16, 18): 27 (31, 33, 37) sts.

Row 5: K1, SSK, K9 (11, 12, 14), DD, K9 (11, 12, 14), K2tog, K1: 23 (27, 29, 33) sts.

Row 6: K10 (12, 13, 15), DD, K10 (12, 13, 15): 21 (25, 27, 31) sts.

Row 8: K1, SSK, K6 (8, 9, 11), DD, K6 (8, 9, 11), K2tog, K1: 17(21, 23, 27) sts.

Row 9: K7 (9, 10, 12), DD, K7 (9, 10, 12): 15 (19, 21, 25) sts.

Row 11: K1, SSK, K3 (5, 6, 8), DD, K3 (5, 6, 8), K2tog, K1: 11 (15, 17, 21) sts.

Row 12: K4 (6, 7, 9), DD, K4 (6, 7, 9): 9 (13, 15, 19) sts.

For size S only:

Row 14: K1, SSK, DD, K2tog, K1: 5 sts.

Row 15: K1, DD, K1: 3 sts.

Row 16: DD. Fasten off.

For sizes M, L, XL only:

Row 14: K1, SSK, K2 (3, 5), DD, K2 (3, 5), K2tog, K1: 9 (11, 15) sts.

For sizes M only:

Row 15: K1, SSK, DD, K2tog, K1: 5 sts.

Row 16: K1, DD, K1: 3 sts.

Row 17: DD. Fasten off.

Continue for sizes L and XL only:

Row 15: K1, SSK, K1 (3), DD, K1 (3), K2tog, K1: 7 (11) sts.

For size L only:

Row 16: SSK, DD, K2tog: 3 sts.

Row 17: DD. Fasten off.

For size XL only:

Row 16: K1, SSK, K1, DD, K1, K2tog, K1: 7 sts.

Row 17: SSK, DD, K2tog: 3 sts.

Row 18: DD. Fasten off.

Note: Place a stitch marker or safety pin onto Triangle #1. This triangle is the center-back.

Triangle #2

Using B, CO 17 (19, 20, 22) sts and PU 16 (18, 19, 21) sts along right-hand side of Triangle #1: 33 (37, 39, 43) sts.

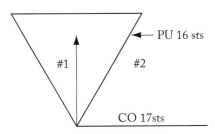

Triangle #3

Using B, PU 16 (18, 19, 21) sts along left-hand side of Triangle #1 and CO 17 (19, 20, 22) sts: 33 (37, 39, 43) sts.

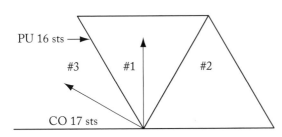

Triangles #2, 4, 6, 8, 10, 12, 14, 16, 18 are worked to the right of Triangle #1 on each succeeding triangle toward the right front. Using A, CO 17 (19, 20, 22) sts and PU 16 (18, 19, 21)sts: 33 (37, 39, 43) sts. See diagram on page 57.

Triangles #3, 5, 7, 9, 11, 13, 15, 17, 19 are worked to the left of Triangle #1 on each succeeding triangle toward the left front. Using A, PU 16 (18, 19, 21) sts and CO 17 (19, 20, 22) sts. See diagram on page 57.

Triangles #1-4 are shown completed below.

Triangle #5

Using A, PU 16 (18, 19, 21) sts along left-hand side of Triangle #3 and CO 17 (19, 20, 22) sts: 33 (37, 39, 43) sts.

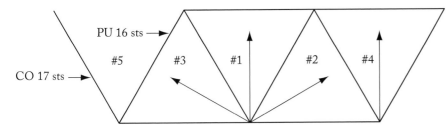

At right front edge, fill in Half-Triangle on the right-hand side of upward pointing Triangle. PU 17 (19, 20, 22) sts.

Rows 1, 4, 7, 10 and 13: Knit across.

Row 2: SSK, K12 (14, 15, 17), K2tog, K1: 15 (17, 18, 20) sts.

Row 3: K13 (15, 16, 18), K2tog: 14 (16, 17, 19) sts.

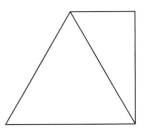

Row 5: K1, SSK, K9 (11, 12, 14), K2tog: 12 (14, 15, 17) sts.

Row 6: SSK, K10 (12, 13, 15): 11 (13, 14, 16) sts.

Row 8: SSK, K6 (8, 9, 11), K2tog, K1: 9 (11, 12, 14) sts.

Row 9: K7 (9, 10, 12), K2tog: 8 (10, 11, 13) sts.

Row 11: K1, SSK, K3 (5, 6, 8), K2tog: 6 (8, 9, 11) sts.

Row 12: SSK, K4 (6, 7, 9): 5 (7, 8, 10) sts.

For size S only:

Row 14: SSK, K2tog, K1: 3 sts.

Row 15: K1, K2tog: 2 sts.

Row 16: SSK: 1 st. Fasten off rem st.

For sizes M, L, XL only:

Row 14: SSK, K2 (3, 5) K2tog, K1: 5 (6, 8) sts.

For size M only:

Row 15: SSK, K2tog, K1: 3 sts.

Row 16: K1, K2tog: 2 sts.

Row 17: SSK: 1 st. Fasten off rem st.

For sizes L and XL only:

Row 15: SSK, K1 (3), K2tog, K1: 4 (6) sts.

For size L only:

Row 16: SSK, K2tog: 2 sts.

Row 17: SSK: 1 st. Fasten off rem st.

TRIANGLE PATCHWORK

For size XL only:

Row 16: SSK, K2, K2tog: 4 sts.

Row 17: SSK, K2tog: 2 sts.

Row 18: SSK: 1 st. Fasten off rem st.

At left front edge, fill in Half-Triangle on the left-hand side of upward pointing Triangle. PU 17 (19, 20, 22) sts.

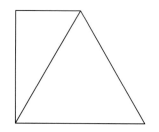

Leave a long tail when casting on. The tail is used to sew the ends of the triangles together.

Rows 1, 4, 7, 10 and 13: Knit across.

Row 2: K1, SSK, K12 (14, 15, 17), K2tog: 15 (17, 18, 20) sts.

Row 3: SSK, K13 (15, 16, 18): 14 (16, 17, 19) sts.

Row 5: SSK, K9 (11, 12, 14), K2tog, K1: 12 (14, 15, 17) sts.

Row 6: K10 (12, 13, 15), K2tog: 11 (13, 14, 16) sts.

Row 8: K1, SSK, K6 (8, 9, 11), K2tog: 9 (11, 12, 14) sts.

Row 9: SSK, K7 (9, 10, 12): 8 (10, 11, 13) sts.

Row 11: SSK, K3 (5, 6, 8), K2tog, K1: 6 (8, 9, 11) sts.

Row 12: K4 (6, 7, 9), K2tog: 5 (7, 8, 10) sts.

For size S only:

Row 14: K1, SSK, K2tog: 3 sts.

Row 15: SSK, K1: 2 sts.

Row 16: K2tog: 1 st. Fasten off rem st.

For sizes M, L and XL only:

Row 14: SSK, K2 (3, 5), K2tog, K1: 5 (6, 8) sts.

For size M only:

Row 15: SSK, K2tog, K1: 3 sts.

Row 16: K1, K2tog: 2 sts.

Row 17: SSK: 1 st. Fasten off rem st.

For sizes L and XL only:

Row 15: SSK, K1 (3), K2tog, K1: 4 (6) sts.

For size L only:

Row 16: SSK, K2tog: 2 sts.

Row 17: SSK: 1 st. Fasten off rem st.

For size XL only:

Row 16: SSK, K2, K2tog: 4 sts.

Row 17: SSK, K2tog: 2 sts.

Row 18: SSK: 1 st. Fasten off rem st.

The completed first row of small triangles, with half-triangles at the ends, should measure about 37 (41, 46¼, 51¾)" side.

The body of the sweater will be constructed in one piece up to the underarm. Continue working as follows:

Row 2: Work the three large triangles first. (Instructions for Large Triangles follow.) Attach one edge of triangle in position on Row 1 as shown in diagram on page 57. Then work the small triangles to fill in the row.

Large Triangle Construction Method:
Follow the same rules as for the small triangle.

Method 1: CO 33 (37, 39, 43) sts and PU 32 (36, 38, 42) sts **or,**

Method 2: PU 32 (36, 38, 42) sts and CO 33 (37, 39, 43) sts **or,**

Method 3: PU 65 (73, 77, 85) sts.

CO 65 (73, 77, 85) sts.

Change color every 2 rows (1 ridge).

Rows 1, 4 and 7: Knit across.

Row 2: K1, SSK, K28 (32, 34, 38), DD, K28 (32, 34, 38), K2tog, K1: 61(69, 73, 81) sts.

Row 3: K29 (33, 35, 39), DD, K29 (33, 35, 39): 59 (67, 71, 79) sts.

Row 5: K1, SSK, K25 (29, 31, 35), DD, K25 (29, 31, 35), K2tog, K1: 55 (63, 67, 75) sts.

Row 6: K26 (30, 32, 36), DD, K26 (30, 32, 36): 53 (61, 65, 73) sts.

Row 8: K1, SSK, K22 (26, 28, 32), DD, K22 (26, 28, 32), K2tog, K1: 49 (57, 61, 69) sts.

Row 9: K23 (27, 29, 33), DD, K23 (27, 29, 33): 47 (55, 59, 67) sts.

Rows 10, 13 and 16: Knit across.

Row 11: K1, SSK, K19 (23, 25, 29), DD, K19 (23, 25, 29), K2tog, K1: 43 (51, 55, 63) sts.

Row 12: K20 (24, 26, 30), DD, K20 (24, 26, 30): 41 (49, 53, 61) sts.

Row 14: K1, SSK, K16 (20, 22, 26), DD, K16 (20, 22, 26), K2tog, K1: 37 (45, 49, 57) sts.

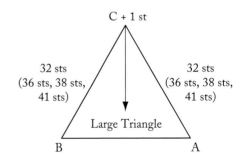

Row 15: K17 (21, 23, 27), DD, K17 (21, 23, 27): 35 (43, 47, 55) sts.

TRIANGLE PATCHWORK

Row 17: K1, SSK, K13 (17, 19, 23), DD, K13 (17, 19, 23), K2tog, K1: 31 (39, 43, 51) sts.

Row 18: K14 (18, 20, 24), DD, K14 (18, 20, 24): 29 (37, 41, 49) sts.

Rows 19, 22 and 25: Knit across.

Row 20: K1, SSK, K10 (14, 16, 20), DD, K10 (14, 16, 20), K2tog, K1: 25 (33, 37, 45) sts.

Row 21: K11 (15, 17, 21), DD, K11 (15, 17, 21): 23 (31, 35, 43) sts.

Row 23: K1, SSK, K7 (11, 13, 17), DD, K7 (11, 13, 17), K2tog, K1: 19 (27, 31, 39) sts.

Row 24: K8 (12, 14, 18), DD, K8 (12, 14, 18): 17 (25, 29, 37) sts.

Row 26: K1, SSK, K4 (8, 10, 14), DD, K4 (8, 10, 14), K2tog, K1: 13 (21, 25, 33) sts.

Row 27: K5 (9, 11, 15), DD, K5 (9, 11, 15): 11 (19, 23, 31) sts.

Row 28 and 31: Knit across.

Row 29: K1, SSK, K1 (5, 7, 11), DD, K1 (5, 7, 11), K2tog, K1: 7 (15, 19, 27) sts.

For size S only:
Row 30: SSK, DD, K2tog: 3 sts.

Row 31: Knit.

Row 32: DD: 1 st. Fasten off rem st.

For sizes M, L and XL only:
Row 30: K6 (8, 12), DD, K6 (8, 12): 13 (17, 25) sts.

Row 31: Knit across

Row 32: K1, SSK, K2 (4, 8), DD, K2 (4, 8), K2tog, K1: 9 (13, 21) sts.

Row 33: K3 (5, 9), DD, K3 (5, 9): 7 (11, 19) sts.

Rows 34 and 35: Knit across.

For size M only:
Row 36: SSK, DD, K2tog: 3 sts.

Row 37: Knit across.

Row 38: DD: 1 st. Fasten off rem st.

For sizes L and XL only:
Row 36: K1, SSK, K1 (5), DD, K1, (5), K2tog, K1: 7 (15) sts.

Row 37: Knit across.

For size L only:
Row 38: SSK, DD, K2tog: 3 sts.

Row 39: DD: 1 st. Fasten off rem st.

For size XL only:
Row 38: K1, SSK, K3, DD, K3, K2tog, K1: 11 sts.

Row 39: K4, DD, K4: 9 sts.

Rows 40 and 43: Knit across.

Row 41: K1, SSK, DD, K2tog: 5 sts.

Row 42: K1, DD, K1: 3 sts.

Row 44: DD: 1 st. Fasten off rem st.

Now continue with Row 3, working small triangles to fill in the row.

Fill in the front edge on each end with a Long Triangle (directions follow.)

To Work Long Triangles for Front Edge:
(Triangles 51, 52, 81 and 85 on diagram on page 57.)

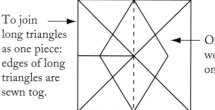

To join long triangles as one piece: edges of long triangles are sewn tog.

Or, you may work them as one piece

For size S only:
PU 33 sts.

Rows 1, 4, 5, 8, 9, 12: Knit across.

Row 2: SSK, K13, DD, K13, K2tog: 29 sts.

Row 3: SSK, K11, DD, K11, K2tog: 25 sts.

Row 6: SSK, K9, DD, K9, K2tog: 21 sts.

Row 7: SSK, K7, DD, K7, K2tog: 17 sts.

Row 10: SSK, K5, DD, K5, K2tog: 13 sts.

Row 11: SSK, K3, DD, K3, K2tog: 9 sts.

Row 13: SSK, K1, DD, K1, K2tog: 5 sts.

Row 14: K1, DD, K1: 3 sts.

Row 15: DD: 1 st. Fasten off rem st.

For sizes M, L and XL only: PU 37 (41, 45) sts.

Rows 1, 4, 5, 8, 9 and 12: Knit across.

Row 2: SSK, K15 (17, 19), DD, K15 (17, 19), K2tog: 33 (37, 41) sts.

Row 3: SSK, K13 (15, 17), DD, K13 (15, 17), K2tog: 29 (33, 37) sts.

Row 6: SSK, K11 (13, 15), DD, K11 (13, 15), K2tog: 25 (29, 33) sts.

Row 7: SSK, K9 (11, 13), DD, K9 (11, 13), K2tog: 21 (25, 29) sts.

Row 10: SSK, K7 (9, 11), DD, K7 (9, 11), K2tog: 17 (21, 25) sts.

Row 11: SSK, K5 (7, 9), DD, K5 (7, 9), K2tog: 13 (17, 21) sts.

For size M only:
Row 13: SSK, K3, DD, K3, K2tog: 9 sts.

Row 14: SSK, K1, DD, K1, K2tog: 5 sts.

Row 15: K1, DD, K1: 3 sts.

Row 16: DD: 1 st. Fasten off rem st.

For size L only:
Rows 13 and 16: Knit across.

TRIANGLE PATCHWORK

Row 14: SSK, K5, DD, K5, K2tog: 13 sts.

Row 15: SSK, K3, DD, K3, K2tog: 9 sts.

Row 17: SSK, K1, DD, K1, K2tog: 5 sts.

Row 18: K1, DD, K1: 3 sts.

Row 19: DD: 1 st. Fasten off rem st.

For size XL only:

Rows 13, 16 and 17: Knit across.

Row 14: SSK, K7, DD, K7, K2tog: 17 sts.

Row 15: SSK, K5, DD, K5, K2tog: 13 sts.

Row 18: SSK, K3, DD, K3, K2tog: 9 sts.

Row 19: SSK, K1, DD, K1, K2tog: 5 sts.

Row 20: K1, DD, K1: 3 sts.

Row 21: DD: 1 st. Fasten off rem st.

Now work Row 4, with small triangles to work to the underarms.

Bottom Band

With larger needle and A, with right side facing, PU 16 (18, 19, 21) sts from each triangle, then PU 1 st at each triangle intersection to avoid having a hole. Knit back one row. Cut A. Count your sts.

Back

Use st markers to indicate the center 12 (13 1/2, 14 3/4, 17 1/4)".

Attach B, then knit across row and inc or dec evenly across until you have 148 (164, 185, 207) sts. Knit each row until band measures 3". BO.

Back Yoke (for all sizes)

With larger size needle and A, PU 16 (18, 19, 21) sts across each triangle, 8 (9, 10, 11) sts across each half triangle and 1 st at each triangle intersection: 51 (57, 51, 67) sts. *Note: If you pick up sts across each triangle only, you will notice a small hole. The extra st is used to eliminate the hole. Do not cut yarn.*

After picking up the sts, knit one row. Count your sts. Attach B. On next right-side row, knit across and inc or dec evenly across until you have 48 (54, 59, 69) sts.

Work in Garter St Stripe pattern (knit 2 rows Color A and 2 rows Color B) until armholes measure 8 (8 3/4, 9 1/2, 10)". Do not BO. Place sts on a st holder or piece of yarn. Shoulders are knitted tog using a 3-needle BO (see page 126).

Right Front

Row 5: See diagram on page 57 for placement of Triangles 79 through 81. Work these triangles.

With larger needle and A, PU 16 (18, 19, 21) sts across triangle, 8 (9, 10, 11) sts across half-triangle and 1 st at triangle intersection to eliminate the hole. Do not cut yarn.

After picking up the sts, knit one row. Count your sts. Attach B, on next right-side row, knit across and inc or

Row 5: See diagram (on page 57) for placement of Triangles 72 through 78. Work these triangles.

TRIANGLE PATCHWORK

dec evenly across until you have 24 (27, 28, 34) sts.

Work in Garter St Stripe Pattern (knit 2 rows Color A and 2 rows Color B) until armhole measures 5 (5 1/4, 6 1/4, 6 1/4)". Do not BO.

Shape neck

At neck edge, BO 6 (6, 7, 7) sts. Dec 1 st at neck edge every other row until 11 (12, 13, 17) sts rem.

Work even until armhole measures same as back. Knit shoulders tog using a 3-needle BO (see page 126).

Left Front

Row 5: See diagram on page 57 for placement of Triangles 83 through 86. Work these triangles.

Complete to correspond to right front, reversing shaping.

Sleeves (make 2)

Note: *Sleeves are worked in Garter St Stripes(knit 2 rows Color A and 2 rows*

Color B). The sleeves are attached at the underarm without sewing.

Knit-in Sleeve Cap

With right-side facing, with larger needle and A, PU 32 (36, 38, 42) sts across underarm edge. Continue to PU 64 (70, 76, 80) sts evenly along armhole edge. Turn work.

Row 1 wrong side: Wyif, sl first st from right to left, knit across until 1 sleeve st rem, knit next 2 sts tog (1 st from sleeve and 1 st from underarm). Turn work.

Row 2 (right side): Attach B, wyib, sl first st from right to left, knit across until 1 sleeve st rem, knit next 2 sts tog (1 st from sleeve and 1 st from underarm). Turn work.

Rep Rows 1 and 2 until all of the underarm sts are worked. Continue working sleeves back and forth in rows using the Garter St Stripe pattern.

Body of sleeve

Dec 1 st each side every 11 rows (or at beg of every sixth garter st ridge) until underarm seam measures approx 14" or 3" less than desired sleeve length, ending by working last row with A. Count the sts. Cut A.

With smaller needle, continue with B and dec evenly across on next row until you have 36 (38, 44, 48) sts. Knit every row for 3". BO. Leave a long tail to sew the sleeve seam.

Neck Band

Using A and smaller needles, PU 1 st for each BO st, PU 1 st for each garter st ridge, PU 1 st at shoulder, knit across back sts, PU 1 st at shoulder, PU 1 st for each garter stitch ridge, PU 1 st for each BO st. Knit 1 row. Cut A and attach B. Knit neck band for approximately 1". BO all sts.

Button Band

With B, work the left front button band first.

Step 1: Measure the length of the center front, including the bottom band and neckband.

Step 2: Multiply the answer above by the st gauge for smaller needles (4 1/2 sts = 1").

Step 3: The number of sts to pick up evenly for the button band is the final answer in Step 2.

With smaller needles, work the left front button band for approx 1 1/2". BO.

Buttonhole Band:

With B, work the right front buttonhole band.

PU same number of sts as for left front button band.

When band measures 3/4", work seven buttonholes (K2tog, YO) evenly spaced, making sure first and last buttonholes are placed at least 1/2" to 3/4" from top and bottom of sweater.

On next row, knit across all sts and YO's.

Knit until band measures approx 1 1/2". BO.

Sew on buttons.

TO THE POINT

Designed by Donna Druchunas

A creative pointed trim adds interest to this wear-everywhere tank top.

TO THE POINT

SIZES	Small	Medium	Large
Body Bust Measurements	29"- 31"	32"- 34"	35"- 37"
Finished Bust Measurements	33"	36 "	39"

Note: Instructions are written for size Small; changes for sizes Medium and Large are in parentheses.

Materials

Medium weight cotton boucle yarn
  12 (12, 16) oz variegated
Note: Photographed model made with Cherry Tree Hill Cotton Boucle Mini, Spanish Moss
Tapestry needle
Size 9 (5.5mm) knitting needles (or size required for gauge)
16" Size 9 (5.5mm) circular needle

Gauge

16 sts = 4"

INSTRUCTIONS

BACK

Pointed edge:

*With straight knitting needles, CO 2 sts.

Row 1: K2.

Rows 2 through 10 (11, 12): YO, knit to end: 11 (12, 13) sts.

Cut yarn. Rep from * until you have 6 triangles on needle.

Turn and knit across all sts to connect triangles: 66 (72, 78) sts.

BODY

Knit every row on 66 (72, 78) sts until piece measures 9 1/2 (10 1/2, 11 1/2)" from CO at points of triangles.

SHAPE ARMHOLES

BO 4 sts at beg of next 2 rows, then BO 2 sts at beg of following 4 rows. Dec 1 st at beg of next 8 rows: 42 (48, 54) sts. Work even in garter st until armhole measures 4 1/2".

Last Row: K16 (19, 22) sts. BO center 10 sts, k16 (19, 22) sts.

NECK SHAPING

Work each shoulder separately. Continuing in knit, BO 2 sts at neck edge twice, then dec 1 st at neck edge every other row twice: 10 (13, 16) sts. Work even until armhole measures 8 1/2 (9, 9 1/2)". Bind off rem sts.

Attach yarn to neck edge of other shoulder and rep shaping.

FRONT
Work as for Back.

FINISHING
Sew shoulder and side seams.

Armhole bands
With right side facing and circular needle, beginning at underarm seam, pick up approx 66 (70, 74) sts evenly around armhole. Knit 3 rows. BO loosely. Sew armband seam.

Rep for second armhole band.

Neckband
With right side facing and circular needle, beginning at left shoulder seam, pick up approx 84 (92, 100) sts evenly around neck. Knit 3 rows. BO loosely. Sew small seam at left shoulder.

Weave in all ends.

LOG CABIN THROW

Designed by Nazanin S. Fard

The traditional Log Cabin quilt pattern is adapted here and executed in shades of rose, making a very cozy throw.

Size
Approx 48" x 48"

Materials
Worsted (medium) weight yarn
3 1/2 oz. Burgundy (A)
7 oz. Medium Antique Rose (B)
7 oz. Light Antique Rose (C)
10 1/2 oz. Pale Antique Rose (D)
14 oz. Natural (E)
Note: *Photographed model made with Bernat® Berella® 4, #08927 Burgundy, #08816 Medium Antique Rose, #08815 Light Antique Rose, Pale Antique Rose, #08940 Natural*
Size 8 (5 mm) knitting needles (or size required for gauge)
Size G (4 mm) crochet hook

Gauge
16 sts = 4"

BLOCK (Make 36):
Instruction for each block is given in sections. For placement of each section, follow **Fig 1** on page 75.

Section 1: Start by working the center section. With A, CO 10 sts. Knit 16 rows.

Section 2: Change to B, knit 10 rows. BO all sts loosely to last st. Leave last st on needle.

Section 3: With right side facing and B, pick up 13 sts from the side of sections 2 and 1. With the st already on needle you will have 14 sts. Knit 9 rows. BO all sts to last st loosely. Leave last st on needle.

Section 4: With right side facing and C, pick up 14 sts from the side of sections 3 and 1. With the st already on needle you will have 15 sts. Knit 9 rows. BO all sts to last st loosely. Leave last st on needle.

Section 5: With right side facing and C, pick up 19 sts from the side of sections 4, 1, 2. With the st already on needle you will have 20 sts. Knit 9 rows. BO all sts to last st loosely. Leave last st on needle.

Section 6: With right side facing and D, pick up 20 sts from the side of sections 5, 2, 3. With the st already on needle you will have 21 sts. Knit 9 rows. BO all sts to last st loosely. Leave last st on needle.

Section 7: With right side facing and D, pick up 24 sts from the side of sections 6, 3, 4. With the st already on needle you will have 25 sts. Knit 9 rows. BO all sts to last st loosely. Leave last st on needle.

Section 8: With right side facing and E, pick up 25 sts from the side of sections 7, 4, 5. With the st already on needle you will have 26 sts. Knit 9 rows. BO all sts to last st loosely. Leave last st on needle.

Section 9: With right side facing and E, pick up 29 sts from the side of sections 8, 5, 6. With the st already on needle you will have 30 sts. Knit 9 rows. BO all sts. Fasten off.

FINISHING

To join blocks, follow **Fig 2** on page 75 as follows:

Place the right side of two blocks together as shown in diagram. Using matching color yarn and crochet hook, sl st blocks together.

With right side of throw facing you and crochet hook work as follows:

Rnd 1: Ch 1, sc in every st around throw, end with sl st into the first ch.

Rnd 2: Ch 1, reverse sc (working from left to right) in every sc around the throw. Fasten off.

Block throw to size if necessary.

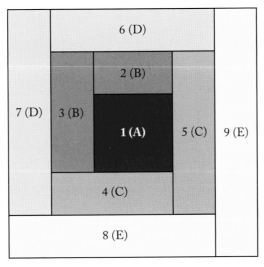

Fig 1

Fig 2

CALYPSO SWEATER

Designed by Diane Moyer

The perfect stash buster project! You can find a way to use whatever is in your stash whether you have whole skeins or just a few delightful pieces which can be used to create your own yarns.

CALYPSO SWEATER

This is a great stash buster sweater. The sweater uses five solid colors, listed as MC, A, B, C, D. For the rest of the sweater, you create your own yarn, called "Magic Yarn". Choose one or two multi colored yarns that you like. Then choose other solid and multi colored yarns in many different textures to go with them. The more variety, the better.

SIZES	Small	Medium	Large
Body Bust Measurements	32"- 34"	36"- 38"	40"- 42"
Finished Bust Measurements	38"	42"	46"

Note: Instructions are written for size Small; changes for sizes Medium and Large are in parentheses.

Materials
Dk weight cotton yarn
- 7 (7, 9) ounces turquoise (MC)
- 3.5 ounces purple (A)
- 3.5 ounces orange (B)
- 1.75 ounces green (C)
- 1.75 ounces pink (D)
- 20 ounces novelty yarns (MY)

Note: Photographed model made with Tahki Stacy Charles Cotton Classic II #2062 Turquoise (MC), #2924 Purple (A), #2401 Orange (B); Berroco® Zen™ #8256 Green (C) and Berroco® Glacé™ #2518 Hot Pink (D). The following novelty yarns were used for (MY): Tahki Stacy Charles Rondo #600 Yellow, #5001 Multi; Berroco® Zen #8114 Mikado Mix, Hip Hop #7237 Way Cool; Plymouth Yarn® Colorlash #127 Deep Orange, Patches #5, Palazzi Novelty #352; Crystal Palace Squiggle #9297 Circus and Sirdar Curly Wurly #0683 Chameleon

Size 9 (5.5mm) knitting needles
  (or size required for gauge)
Size 9 (5.5mm) circular needle 29-32" long
  for neck edging
One 1 1/2" button
Stitch markers

Gauge
16 sts = 4" with MC

Stitch Guide

SSK: Slip next 2 stitches as if to knit, insert left needle through front loop of these 2 stitches, from left and knit them together.

PM: Place marker.

SM: Slip marker.

YF: Yarn forward.

MY (Magic Yarn): These sections are created using novelty yarns in various lengths (1 to 2 1/2 yds), randomly tied together using an overhand knot. Leave 2" tails. Combine thin yarns with other thin yarns. Extra thick yarns should not be used for more than a row or two. Leave the knots are on the right side as a design element.

Hint: When preparing the "Magic Yarn" put all the yarns to be used in a basket or box. Grab one strand from each yarn and pull together. Before cutting, tie a bag twisty around the group of yarns so the yarns are together when you make the next magic ball.

INSTRUCTIONS

Note: The sweater is made in sections. Some are attached as they are knit; others are sewn together. Refer to the diagram on page 79 for the order and direction each piece is knit and put together.

Use markers to mark the right side of the work. When picking up stitches along a side, always pick up with the right side facing you. When changing from a solid color section to another color or Magic Yarn section, always do this on the right side.

Since you want the piece to lie flat and have fairly straight edges, depending on the yarn being used, you may need to increase or decrease the number of stitches given. This also applies to row count. It is important that you get the correct measurements for each piece.

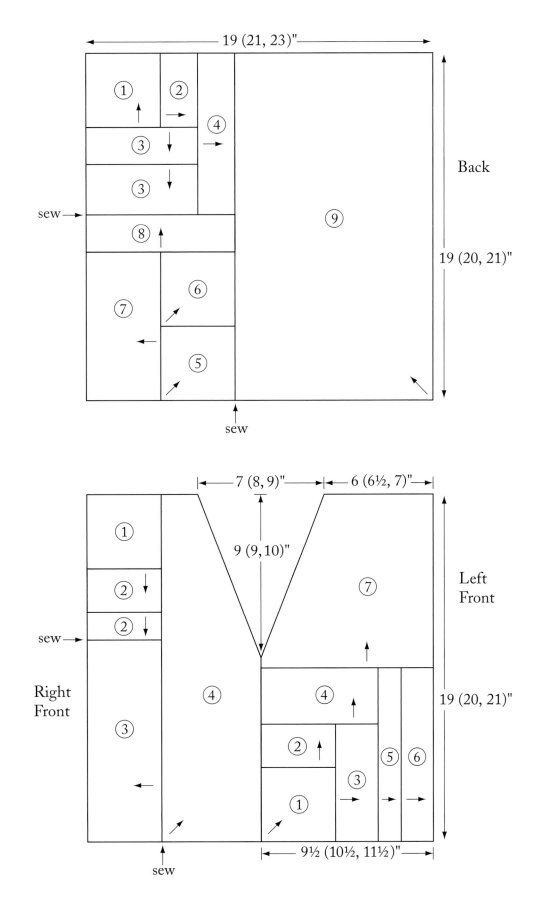

19 (21, 23)"

① ② ④ ③ ③

sew →

⑧

⑨

Back

19 (20, 21)"

⑦ ⑥

⑤

sew

7 (8, 9)" 6 (6½, 7)"

9 (9, 10)"

① ② ②

sew →

Right Front

③

④ ④

② ③

① ⑤ ⑥

⑦

Left Front

19 (20, 21)"

sew

9½ (10½, 11½)"

79

CALYPSO SWEATER

BACK

Piece #1: With MC, CO 16 (18, 20) sts. Knit each row until piece is a 4 (4 1/2, 5)" square. BO.

Piece #2: With MY, pick up 16 (18, 20) sts along the right edge of Piece #1. Knit each row for 2", ending with wrong-side row. BO.

Piece #3: With D, pick up 24 (26, 28) sts along the bottom edge of Pieces #1 and #2. Knit each row for 2", ending with wrong-side row. Cut yarn. Change to MY and continue knitting each row for 3 (2 1/2, 2)" more, ending with wrong-side row. BO.

Piece #4: With A, pick up 36 sts along the right edge of Pieces #1, #2 and #3. Knit each row for 2 (2 1/2, 3)", ending with wrong-side row. BO and set aside this section.

Piece #5: With A, CO 15 (17, 19) sts, PM, CO another 15 (17, 19) sts: 30 (34, 38) sts. Work a mitered square as follows:

Row 1 (wrong side): Knit.

Row 2 (right side): Knit until 2 sts before marker. K2tog, SM, SSK, knit to end: 28 sts. (Mark this side so you will know it's the right side.)

Row 3 and all wrong-side rows: Knit.

Rep Rows 2 and 3 until 2 sts remain, ending by working Row 2.

Last row (wrong side): K2tog. Cut yarn and secure last st.

Piece #6: With B and right side facing, pick up 15 (17, 19) sts along the top edge of Piece #5, PM, and CO another 15 (17, 19) sts: 30 (34, 38) sts.

Make a second mitered square following the directions given for Piece #5, starting with Row 1.

Piece #7: With MY, pick up 30 (34, 38) sts along the left sides of Pieces #5 and #6. Knit each row for 4 (4 1/2, 5)", ending with wrong-side row. BO.

Piece #8: With C, pick up 32 (36, 40) sts along top edge of Piece # 6 and #7. Knit each row for 2", ending with wrong-side row. BO.

Sew this section to the first section using the diagram on page 79 as a guide.

Piece #9: This piece is done on the diagonal. With MC, CO 3 sts. Knit one row.

Row 1 (right side): Inc in first st, K1, inc in last st: 5 sts.

Row 2: Knit.

Row 3: Inc in first st, knit to last st, inc in last st: 7 sts.

Row 4 and all wrong-side rows: Knit.

Row 5: Rep Row 3: 9 sts.

Row 6: Knit. Cut yarn and attach MY.

Continue to inc in the first and last sts of every right-side row and knit evenly across every wrong-side row until you have 55 (59, 63) sts changing the yarns as follows:

MY: 10 (12, 12) rows: 19 (21, 21) sts.

MC: 4 (4, 6) rows: 23 (25, 27) sts.

MY: 6 (8, 8) rows: 29 (33, 35) sts.

MC: 2 (2, 4) rows: 31 (35, 39) sts.

MY: 18 (18, 18) rows: 49 (53, 57) sts.

MC: 6 (6, 6) rows: 55 (59, 63) sts.

The piece should measure 11 (12, 13)" along the bottom edge.

Change to MY.

Shaping the Rectangle

Row 1 (right side): With MY, inc in first st, knit to last 2 sts, K2tog: 55 (59, 63) sts.

Row 2 (wrong side): Knit.

The number of sts will remain the same until the shoulder shaping. Change yarns as follows:

MY: 18 (18, 18) more rows.

MC: 12 (12, 12) rows.

MY: 10 (10, 10) rows.

The piece should measure 19 (20, 21)" along the right edge with right side facing.

Decreasing for the Shoulder

Row 1 (right side): Continuing with MY, K2tog, knit to last 2 sts, K2 tog: 53 (57, 61) sts.

Row 2 (wrong side): Knit.

Rep the last 2 rows until 3 sts remain, changing yarns as follows:

MY: 2 additional rows: 51 (55, 59) sts.

MC: 2 rows: 49 (53, 57) sts.

MY: 4 (6, 8) rows: 45 (47, 49) sts.

MC: 2 rows: 43 (45, 47) sts.

MY: 6 (8, 10) rows: 37 (37, 37) sts

MC: 4 rows: 33 (33, 33) sts.

MY: 14 rows: 19 (19, 19) sts.

MC: 15 rows: 4 (4, 4) sts.

Last row (wrong side): Sl 1, K3tog, pass sl st over. Fasten off.

RIGHT FRONT

Piece #1: With B, CO 15 (17, 19) sts, PM, CO another 15 (17, 19) sts: 30 (34, 38) sts. Make a mitered square, following the directions given for the back.

Piece #2: With D, pick up 15 (17, 19) sts along the bottom edge of Piece #1 and knit each row for 2 1/2 (2 1/2, 3)". Cut yarn. Attach C and knit each row for 1 1/2 (2, 2)", ending with a wrong-side row. BO and set aside.

Piece #3: With MC, cast on 44 sts. Knit each row for 4 (4 1/2, 5)", ending with a wrong-side row. BO.

Sew Pieces #1 and #2 to the top edge of Piece #3, using the schematic as a guide. Set aside.

Piece # 4: This piece is done on the diagonal, similar to the back section. With MY, CO 3 sts. Knit 1 row.

Row 1 (right side): Inc in first st, K1, inc in last st: 5 sts.

Row 2 (wrong side): Knit.

Row 3: Inc in first st, knit to last st, inc in last st:7 sts.

Row 4: Knit.

Rep these last 2 rows, changing yarns as follows:

CALYPSO SWEATER

MY: 12 additional rows: 19 (19, 19) sts.

MC: 2 rows: 21 (21, 21) sts.

MY: 4 (6, 8) rows: 25 (27, 29) sts.

MC: 4 rows: 29 (31, 33) sts.

Piece should measure 5 1/2 (6, 6 1/2)" along bottom edge.

Shaping the Center Front
PM at center front edge.

Row 1 (right side): With MY, K2tog, knit to last st, inc in last st: 29 (31, 33) sts.

Row 2 (wrong side): Knit.

Rep Rows 1 and 2, changing colors as directed, until the front edge measures 10 (11, 11)". The st count will remain 29 (31, 33) sts until you reach this measurement. Change yarns as follows:

MY: 10 more rows.

MC: 10 (14, 14) rows.

MY: 18 (16, 16) rows.

MC: 4 (6, 6) rows.

MY: 6 rows.

If the right edge of the piece does not measure 10 (11, 11)", continue working until measurement is reached.

Decreasing for the Neck
PM at right edge with the right side facing

Row 1 (right side): Continuing with MY, BO 2 sts at beg of row, knit to last st, inc in last st: 28 (30, 32) sts.

Row 2 (wrong side): Knit to last st, YF, sl last st.

Row 3 (right side): Sl first 2 sts, pass first st over second st, K1, sl st already on right needle over the one just knit: 2 sts BO. (This eliminates the stair step effect.) Knit to last st, inc in last st: 27 (29, 31) sts.

Rep last 2 rows changing yarns as follows:

MY: 8 rows above marker: 25 (27, 29) sts.

MC: 4 rows: 23 (25, 27) sts.

MY: 8 rows: 19 (21, 23) sts. Piece should measure 19 (20, 21)" along left side.

Decreasing for the Shoulder

Continue using MY and dec as follows:

Row 1 (right side): With MY BO 2 sts at beg of row (as already established), knit to last 2 sts, K2tog.

Row 2 (wrong side): Knit.

Rep Rows 1 and 2 until 4 (6, 8) sts remain, ending with wrong-side row.

Last Row (right side): BO 1 (3, 5) sts, K2tog, sl first st over K2tog st. Fasten off.

Sew first section to left side of Piece #4. Refer to the diagram on page 79 as needed.

LEFT FRONT

Piece #1: With MC, CO 15 (17, 19) sts, PM, CO another 15 (17, 19) sts: 30 (34, 38) sts. Make a mitered square following the directions given for the back.

Piece #2: With A, pick up 15 (17, 19) sts along the top of Piece #1. Knit each row for 2", ending with a wrong-side row. BO.

Piece #3: With MY, pick up 23 (25, 27) sts along the right edge of Pieces #1 and #2. Knit each row for 2 1/2", ending with a wrong-side row. BO.

Piece #4: With B, pick up 25 (27, 29) sts along the top edge of Pieces #2 and #3. Knit each row for 3 (3 1/2, 3)", ending with a wrong-side row. BO.

Piece #5: With C, pick up 36 (38, 40) sts along the right edge of Pieces #3 and #4. Knit each row for 1 (1 1/2, 1 1/2)". Cut yarn.

Piece #6: Attach MC. Knit each row for another 2 (2, 2 1/2)", ending with a wrong-side row. BO.

Piece #7: With MY, pick up 38 (42, 46) sts along the top of Pieces #4, #5 and #6. Knit each row for

1" or until piece measures 10 (11, 11)" from bottom, ending with a wrong-side row. PM at neck edge.

CALYPSO SWEATER

Decrease for the Neck

Row 1 (right side): Knit.

Row 2 (wrong side): BO 1 st, knit to end: 37 (41, 45) sts.

Row 3 (right side): Knit to last st, YF, sl last st.

Row 4 (wrong side): Sl first 2 sts to right needle, sl first st over second st (1 st BO), knit to end: 36 (40, 44) sts.

Rows 5 and 6: Knit.

Rep rows 3 through 6 until 21 (25, 29) sts remain, changing colors as follows:

MY: 6 rows: 34 (38, 42) sts.

MC: 4 rows: 33 (37, 41) sts.

MY: 6 rows: 32 (36, 40) sts.

MC: 2 rows: 31 (35, 39) sts.

MY: 10 rows: 29 (33, 37) sts.

MC: 10 rows: 26 (30, 34) sts.

MY: 8 rows: 24 (28, 32) sts.

MC: 2 rows: 24 (28, 32) sts.

MY: 12 rows: 21 (25, 29) sts.

Continue to work even with MY until left front measures 19 (20, 21)" from the bottom or the same as the back. BO remaining sts.

SLEEVES

Sew the shoulder seams together. Measure 8 1/2 (9, 9 1/2)" down from the shoulder seam on front and back. Mark both places. With MC, pick up 68 (72, 76) sts between the markers.

Row 1 (wrong side): Knit.

Row 2 (right side): K1, K2tog, knit to last 3 sts, SSK, K1: 66, (70, 74) sts.

Rep last 2 rows 2 more times until 62 (66, 70) sts remain. Knit each row for 1 1/2" from picked up sts, ending with wrong-side row. BO.

NECKLINE

With MC and circular needle, start at the bottom right front, pick up sts evenly until 1/2" from beginning of neck decreasing: approximately 38 (42, 42) sts. Turn and CO 18 sts. BO the sts you just CO. Fold this strip, place behind the front edge, and pick up next st through the front edge and the end of the BO sts. (This strip becomes the buttonhole loop and is now attached to the sweater.) Pick up 1 more st to reach the marker where the neckline decreasing began: approximately 40 (44, 44) sts. Pick up 34 (34, 38) sts along right neckline, 32 (32, 36) st along back, 34 (34, 38) sts along left neckline and 40 (44, 44) sts along left front: 180 (188, 200) sts. Knit one row. BO all sts.

FINISHING

Sew the side seams together and weave in unwanted ends. Sew on the button.

JELLY BAGS

Designed by Kathleen Greco

Made with the innovative Jelly Yarn®, these colorful bags are quick to make and fun to knit. They are perfect gifts for anyone who would like a little color in her life.

JELLY BAGS

Size
5" high x 8" wide

Materials

For lime-green bag
Bulky yarn
   200 grams, 85 yards blue (A)
   200 grams, 85 yards lime (B)
Note: Photographed model made with Bulky Jelly Yarn®, Blue-Taffy (A) and Lemon-Lime Ice (B)

For pink bag
Bulky yarn
   200 grams, 85 yards black (A)
   200 grams, 85 yards pink (B)
Note: Photographed model made with Bulky Jelly Yarn®, Black Licorice (A) and Pink Parfait (B)

For raspberry bag
   200 grams, 85 yards red (A)
   200 grams, 85 yards raspberry (B)
Note: Photographed model made with Bulky Jelly Yarn®, Wild Cherry Red (A) and Raspberry Sorbet (B)

For all bags
Two 1/2" shank buttons
Size 11 (8 mm) knitting needles

Gauge
10 sts = 4"

Stitch Guide

Inc: Knit into front and back of st: increase made.

Notes on working with Jelly Yarn®

1. Pull yarn from the center and the outside of the ball to knit 2 strands together.

2. Wipe a vinyl protectant (i.e. Vinylex) along the stitches on metal needles for easy glide.

3. Tie a secure knot with yarn by pulling strands very tight until they stretch; then release, repeat to make a double knot.

4. Do not weave in loose ends. Instead, tie a hidden secure double knot and trim ends.

5. Leave an 8" strand at the end of each CO and BO row for sewing seams.

INSTRUCTIONS

FIRST TOP BORDER

Starting at top with two strands of Color A held tog, CO 22 sts, leaving a 8" strand for sewing the side seams.

Row 1 (right side): Knit across.

Repeat Row 1 until piece measures 2" from CO edge, ending by working a wrong-side row. Cut Color A and join 2 strands of Color B, leaving an 8" strand for sewing the side seams.

BODY

Row 1 (right side): With Color B, K1, K2tog, knit across to last 3 sts, K2tog, K1: 20 sts.

Row 2: Knit.

Repeat Row 2 until piece measures 8" from CO edge of Color B, ending by working a wrong-side row. Cut Color B and join 2 strands of Color A.

SECOND TOP BORDER

Row 1 (right side): With Color A, K1, inc, knit to last 2 sts, inc, K1: 22 sts.

Row 2: Knit.

Repeat Row 2 until entire piece measures 12" from first CO row, ending by working a wrong-side row.

BO very loosely.

STRAP

With 2 strands of Color A held tog, CO 4 sts.

Knit for 13" or desired length for strap. BO loosely.

FINISHING

With right sides tog, fold purse in half and sew side seams with matching yarn strands. Fold Top Border edges over about 1". Sew strap to right Top Border. Straighten strap and repeat for other side.

Thread button with one strand of Color A. Center button on front side and pull strands through 2 knit layers. Tie a secure double knot on inside of bag. Repeat for back side.

Make a loop with 1 strand and wrap around each button for closure. Tie a double knot.

Fill purse with a light weight and hang overnight to straighten strap and form shape.

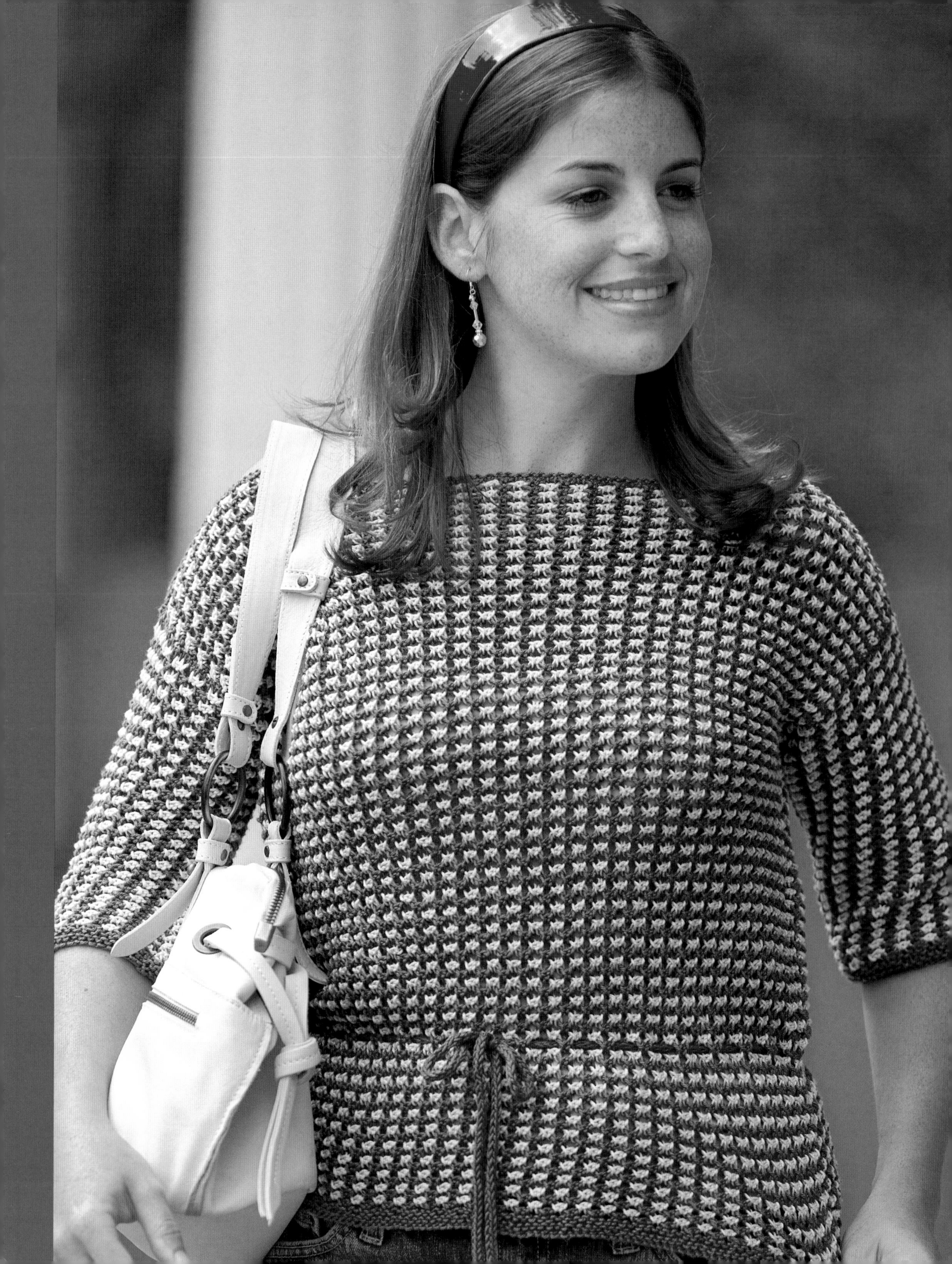

ON THE TOWN

This innovative stitch pattern creates a T-top that could take you just about anywhere your busy schedule might demand. Dress it up or dress it down as you please.

ON THE TOWN

SIZES	Small	Medium	Large
Body Bust Measurements	34"	38"	40"
Finished Bust Measurements	38"	42"	44"

Note: Instructions are written for size Small; changes for sizes Medium and Large are in parentheses.

Materials

Sport or DK weight light worsted
  8 3/4 oz blue (A)
  7 oz natural (B)
Note: Photographed model made with Patons® Grace #60104 Azure (A) and #60008 Natural (B)
Size 6 (4 mm) knitting needles
  (or size required for gauge)
Two double point Size 6 (4 mm) knitting needles

Gauge

21 sts = 4" in pattern

Stitch Guide

Pattern Stitch

Note: When changing colors, do not cut yarn. Carry unused yarn loosely along edge.

Row 1 (right side): With A, knit.

Row 2: K2; *YO, sl 1, K2, pass sl st over K2 sts; rep from * to last st, K1.

Row 3: With B, Knit.

Row 4: K1; *sl 1, K2, pass sl st over K2 sts, YO; rep from * to last 2 sts, K2.

Rep Rows 1 through 4 for patt.

INSTRUCTIONS

FRONT

Starting at lower edge with A, CO 102 (111, 117) sts and knit 4 rows.

Then work in patt until piece measures 18 (19, 20)" from CO edge, ending with Row 2 in A.

Last Row: With A, knit 1 row.

BO loosely.

BACK

Work same as front.

SLEEVES

Starting at lower edge with A, CO 63 (63, 72) sts and

knit 4 rows. Then work in patt until piece measures approximately 9 (9, 10)", from CO row, ending by working Row 1 in A.

Last Row: With A, knit 1 row.

BO loosely.

FINISHING

Sew shoulder seams, leaving a center opening of approximately 10" for boat neck opening.

Sew in sleeves, placing middle of sleeve at shoulder seam.

Sew sides and underarm seam. Weave in all loose ends.

CORD

With blue, CO 3 sts on one double-point needle.

Row 1: With second double-point, K3; do not turn. Slide sts to opposite end of needle.

Row 2: Take yarn around the back side of sts and with other needle, K3; do not turn. Slide sts to opposite end of needle.

Rep Rows 1 and 2 until cord is approximately 45" long. K3tog. Cut yarn and weave in all ends. At waist feed the cord through the holes in the patt.

LINEAR EFFECT

Designed by Nazanin S. Fard

Rows of white stripes add an eye-catching appeal to this charming sweater.

LINEAR EFFECT

SIZES	Small	Medium	Large
Body Bust Measurements	34"- 36"	38"- 40"	42"- 44"
Finished Bust Measurements	40"	44"	48"

Note: Instructions are written for size Small; changes for sizes Medium and Large are in parentheses.

Materials

Bulky weight fancy yarn
  22 3/4 (24, 25, 29 3/4) oz blue (A)
Bulky weight yarn
  7 oz. natural (B)
Note: Photographed model made with Bernat® Frenzy #55134 Mod Marine (A) and Bernat® Softee Chunky #39008 Natural (B)
Size 16 tapestry needle
Four 3/4" buttons, royal blue and gold
Stitch marker
Size 9 (5.5 mm) knitting needles
40" Size 10 1/2 (6.5 mm) circular knitting needle
  (or size required for gauge)

Gauge

12 sts = 4" with larger needle

Stitch Guide

Pattern Stitch

Rows 1 through 10: With A, knit.

Rows 11 and 12: With B, knit.

Rep rows 1 through 12 for patt.

Cable Cast-on for end of row

Step 1: Insert right-hand needle between the last 2 stitches, wrap yarn around needle, pull through and place the live stitch on left-hand needle.

Step 2: Repeat step 1 as many times necessary.

One-row buttonhole: Knit or sl 2 sts onto right needle and sl 2nd st over first, knit or sl another st to right needle and sl 2nd st over first (2 sts BO), sl rem st on left needle back to left needle and CO on 2 sts, knit across sts.

INSTRUCTIONS

LEFT SLEEVE

Beginning at cuff edge of left sleeve, with B and smaller needles, CO 28 (32, 36) sts. Knit 2 rows. Change to larger circular needle; do not join. Work back and forth in patt, inc 1 st on both sides every 4 rows 9 times, then every 6 rows 7 times: 60 (64, 68) sts. Continue in patt until sleeve measures 17 1/2" from beginning. Cut yarn.

BODY

Continuing in patt and using cable cast-on technique, CO 45 (43, 41) sts on right needle for back; knit back sts, then half of sleeve sts, place marker, knit remaining sleeve sts, then CO 45 (43, 41) sts for left front: 150 sts. Work even for 7 (8, 9)", ending with a wrong-side row.

LEFT FRONT/NECK SHAPING

Row 1 (right side): Work all back sts in patt until marker, attach another ball of yarn and BO 3 sts, work even to end of row.

Row 2 (wrong side): Work all front sts in patt until 2 sts from front neck edge, K2tog. Continue knitting back with other ball.

Repeat rows 1 and 2, 8 times more: 75 sts for back, 39 sts for left front.

Last Row (right side): Knit all back sts, then BO all left front sts.

RIGHT FRONT/NECK SHAPING

Row 1 (wrong side): CO 39 sts for right front. Then with other ball of yarn knit back sts in patt.

Row 2 (right side): Knit all back sts, then with other ball of yarn, cable cast-on 1 st and knit all sts to end of row.

Row 3 (wrong side): Knit all front sts, cable cast-on 3 sts, then with the other ball of yarn knit back sts to end of row.

Repeat rows 2 and 3, 8 times more: 75 sts for back, 75 sts front.

With the first ball of yarn join front and back sts and cut second ball. Work even for 7 (8, 9)", ending with a wrong-side row.

RIGHT SLEEVE:

Row 1 (right side): BO 45 (43, 41) sts, work to end of row.

Row 2 (wrong side): BO 45 (43, 41) sts, work to end of row: 60 (64, 68) sts.

Work in patt dec 1 st on both sides every 6 rows 7 times, then every 4 rows, 9 times: 28 (32, 36) sts. Continue in patt until right sleeve measures same as left sleeve to knit rows at cuff. Change to smaller needles and B. Knit 2 rows. BO all sts loosely.

FINISHING

Sew side seams.

Front Band:

With right side facing, using smaller needles and B, pick up and knit 39 sts from right front to neck edge, 41 sts from neck edge to back, 23 sts from back neck, 41 sts from back to neck edge (left front), 39 sts from neck edge to left front: 183 sts.

Rows 1 through 4: Knit.

Row 5 (buttonhole row): K4, (one-row buttonhole, k9) 3 times, one-row buttonhole, knit to end of row.

Row 6 through 9: Knit.

BO all sts loosely.

Bottom Band:

With right side facing, using smaller needles and B, pick up 130 (143, 156) sts along bottom of jacket.

Rows 1 through 6: Knit.

BO all sts loosely.

Block jacket to size.

Sew buttons opposite buttonholes.

WRAP AROUND VEST

Designed by Rosalie Johnston

This pretty vest is designed in the wrap around style that has become so popular. All "fashinistas" will want this versatile piece in their collections.

WRAP AROUND VEST

SIZES	Small	Medium	Large	X- Large
Body Bust Measurements	28"- 30"	32"- 34"	36"- 38"	40"- 42"
Finished Bust Measurements	31"	35"	40"	44"

Note: Instructions are written for size Small; changes for sizes Medium, Large and X-Large are in parentheses.

Materials

DK weight cotton
   8 (8, 8, 10) oz pink
Note: Photographed model made with S. R. Kertzer Super 10 #3956 Dusty
Size 7 (4.5 mm) knitting needles (or size required for gauge)

Gauge

17 sts and 32 rows = 4"

INSTRUCTIONS

LEFT FRONT

CO 50 (55, 60, 65) sts.

Rows 1 through 33: Knit every row.

Row 34 (wrong side): K2tog, knit across: 49 (54, 59, 64) sts.

Row 35: Knit.

Rows 36 through 70: Rep Rows 34 and 35: 31 (36, 41, 46) sts.

Row 71 (right side): BO 5 (6, 7, 8) sts for armhole, knit to end of row: 26 (30, 34, 38) sts.

Row 72: K2tog, knit across to last 2 sts, K2tog: 24 (28, 32, 36) sts.

Row 73: Knit.

Row 74: Rep Row 72: 22 (26, 30, 34) sts.

Row 75: Knit.

Rows 76 through 87 (93, 99, 105): Rep Rows 34 and 35: 16 (17, 18, 19) sts.

Rows 88 (94, 100, 106) through 126: Knit.

Row 127: BO for shoulder.

RIGHT FRONT

CO 70 (80, 90, 100) sts.

Row 1 (right side): Knit.

Row 2: Knit.

Row 3: K2, YO, K2tog, knit across row.

Rows 4 through 16: Knit.

Row 17: Rep Row 3.

Rows 18 through 34: Knit.

Row 35 (right side): BO 16 (21, 26, 31) sts, knit across row: 54 (59, 64, 69) sts.

Row 36: Knit across to last 2 sts, K2tog: 53 (58, 63, 68) sts.

Row 37: Knit.

Rows 38 through 69: Rep Rows 36 and 37: 37 (42, 47, 52) sts.

Row 70 (wrong side): BO 5 (6, 7, 8) sts, knit across to last 2 sts, K2tog: 31 (35, 39, 43) sts.

Row 71: Knit.

Row 72: K2tog, knit across to last 2 sts, K2tog: 29 (33, 37, 41) sts.

Row 73: Knit.

Row 74: Rep Row 72: 27 (31, 35, 39) sts.

Row 75: Knit.

Rows 76 through 97 (103, 109, 115): Rep Rows 36 and 37: 16 (17, 18, 19) sts.

Rows 98 (104, 110, 116) through 126: Knit.

Row 127: BO.

BACK

Cast on 65 (75, 85, 95) sts.

Rows 1 through 69: Knit.

Row 70 (wrong side): BO 5 (6, 7, 8) sts, knit across: 60 (69, 78, 87) sts.

Row 71 (right side): BO 5 (6, 7, 8) sts, knit across: 55 (63, 71, 79) sts.

Row 72: K2tog, knit across to last 2 sts, K2tog: 53 (61, 69, 77) sts.

Row 73: Knit.

Row 74: Rep Row 72: 51 (59, 67, 75) sts.

Rows 75 through 120: Knit.

Row 121 (right side): K16 (17, 18, 19) sts for right shoulder, BO 19 (25, 31, 37) sts for back neck, K16 (17, 18, 19) sts for left shoulder.

LEFT SHOULDER

Row 122 (wrong side): K16 (17, 18, 19) left shoulder sts only; leave other sts unworked on needle (right shoulder).

Rows 123 through 126: Knit these 16 (17, 18, 19) sts.

Row 127: BO 16 (17, 18, 19) sts.

RIGHT SHOULDER

Rows 122 (wrong side): Attach yarn to right shoulder and K16 (17, 18, 19) unworked sts.

WRAP AROUND VEST

Rows 123 through 126: Knit these 16 (17, 18, 19) sts.

Row 127: BO 16 (17, 18, 19) sts.

ASSEMBLY

Sew shoulder seams. Sew side seams.

TIES (Cords)

Side Cords (make 2): CO 2 sts, leaving about a 12"-long tail for sewing. *Sl 1 st as to knit, K1; rep from * until cord is about 13" long; leaving extra yarn to adjust length if needed. BO. Holding both ends of cord, pull slightly to straighten. Sew a cord to vest bottom at each side seam with a few sts for stability. Weave in long end to hold secure.

Right Front Cord: In same manner as side cords, make an 18" cord. Pull slightly to straighten. On right front sew cord to top of lower flap edge at BO row. Weave in ends.

Left front Cord: Pick up 6 sts at mid portion of side edge of lower flap (with first row to be right side).

Rows 1 through 4: Knit.

Row 5: K2tog, 3 times: 3 sts.

Row 6: K2tog, K1: 2 sts.

Row 7: Sl 1 as to knit, K1.

Rep row 7 until cord measures 16" (not counting first 4 rows). Fasten off. Weave in end.

WRAPPING VEST

Put on vest with left flap under right. Take left cord and poke through (slightly enlarging a st) from inside to outside of vest near right side seam, with comfortable fit. Bring cord straight down, about 2" and poke through from outside to inside of vest. Tie in bow with right side seam cord. Wrap right side of vest over left. Take right cord and poke through from outside to inside of vest near left side seam, with comfortable fit. Bring cord straight down and poke through from inside to outside through right flap. Bring cord straight down and poke through vest. Tie in bow with left side seam cord. To remove vest, untie bows and loosen cords. Vest can be removed over head without removing ties.

REVERSIBLE DIAGONAL AFGHAN

Designed by Joyce Renee Wyatt

A very clever sliding technique is used to create an afghan that is reversible with one color becoming more dominant than the other on each side.

REVERSIBLE DIAGONAL AFGHAN

Size
Approximately 42" x 56"

Materials
Worsted weight acrylic
   24 oz multi color blue (A)
   24 oz solid blue (B)
Note: *Photographed model made with Red Heart® Super Saver® #-0984 Shaded Dusk and #3082 Country Blue*
29" size 11 (8 mm) circular knitting needle
   (or size required for gauge)
60" size 11 (8 mm) circular knitting needle

Gauge
12 sts = 4"

Stitch Guide

Reversible Two-Color Garter Stitch

When knitting this afghan, a sliding technique is used so that one color is dominant on each side. A circular needle is required.

CO any number of sts with A. Do not turn. Slide sts to opposite end of needle.

Row 1: With B, knit. Turn.

Row 2: With B, knit. Do not turn. Slide sts to opposite end of needle.

Row 3: With A, knit. Turn.

Row 4: With A, knit. Do not turn. Slide sts to opposite end of needle.

Repeat Rows 1-4 for st patt.

INSTRUCTIONS

Note: *A variation of the above is worked diagonally for the afghan.*

With A, CO 3 sts. Knit 1 row. Slide sts to opposite end of needle.

Row 1: With B, inc 1 st in first st, inc 1 st in next st, knit last st. Turn: 2 sts increased.

Row 2: With B, knit across. Do not turn. Slide sts to opposite end of needle.

Row 3: With A, inc 1 st in first st, knit across until 2 sts rem, inc 1 st in next st, knit last st. Turn: 2 sts increased.

Row 4: With A, knit across. Do not turn. Slide sts to opposite end of needle.

Row 5: With B, inc 1 st in first st, knit across until 2 sts rem, inc 1 st in next st, knit last st. Turn: 2 sts increased.

Row 6: With B, knit across. Do not turn. Slide sts to opposite end of needle.

Row 7: With A, inc 1 st in first st, knit across until 2 sts rem, inc 1 st in next st, knit last st. Turn: 2 sts increased.

Row 8: With A, knit across. Do not turn. Slide sts to opposite end of needle.

Repeat Rows 5 through 8 increasing 2 sts every other row until bottom horizontal edge of blanket measures approx 42" wide or desired width, ending by working Row 8.

Mark the side edge of afghan with a piece of yarn. This is the increase edge of afghan. The opposite edge of afghan is the decrease edge.

Work afghan until the increase edge is 56" long or desired length as follows:

Row 9: With B, inc 1 st in first st, knit across until 2 sts rem, K2tog. Turn.

Row 10: With B, knit across. Do not turn. Slide sts to opposite end of needle.

Row 11: With A, K2tog, knit across until 2 sts rem, inc 1 st in next st, knit last st. Turn.

Row 12: With A, knit across. Do not turn. Slide sts to opposite end of needle.

Repeat Rows 9 through 12 until side edge of afghan measures approx 56" long or desired length, ending by working Row 12.

SQUARING OFF THE TOP EDGE
OF THE AFGHAN

Row 13: With B, K1, K2tog, knit across until 3 sts rem, K2tog, K1. Turn: 2 sts decreased.

Row 14: With B, knit across. Do not turn. Slide sts to opposite end of needle.

Row 15: With A, K1, K2tog, knit across until 3 sts rem, K2tog, K1. Turn: 2 sts decreased.

Row 16: With A, knit across. Do not turn. Slide sts to opposite end of needle.

Repeat Rows 13 through 16 decreasing 2 sts every other row until 3 sts rem. BO rem sts. Weave in ends.

FUN FELTED TOTE

Designed by Donna Druchunas

An unexpected color combination makes a dramatic statement in this easy-to-make tote. Just follow the simple felting instructions and create a bag that is sure to bring nods of approval wherever it is seen.

Size
Approx 14" x 14" x 3 1/2" after felting

Materials
Worsted weight wool yarn,
   630 yds/300g navy
   210 yds/100g periwinkle
   210 yds/100g burgundy
   210 yds/100g purple
   210 yds/100g fuchsia

Note: *Photographed model made with Plymouth Yarn® Galway Worsted #10 Navy, #15 Periwinkle, #117 Fuchsia, #12 Burgundy and Galway Colornep #513 Purple*

Crochet hook
One 1" button
Size 8 (5 mm) knitting needles
   (or size required for gauge)

Gauge
14 sts = 4"

INSTRUCTIONS

SQUARES (Make 8):

Change colors as desired on each square. Start the center with navy and use navy at least once more in each square.

Center: With navy, CO 10 sts. Knit 20 rows (10 ridges). BO 9 sts: 1 st remains on needle.

Change colors. Pick up 9 sts along left side of navy center: 10 sts on needle. Knit 9 rows, ending with a wrong-side row. BO 9 sts: 1 st remains on needle.

Pick up 14 sts along left side of unit: 15 sts on needle. Knit 9 rows, ending with a wrong-side row. BO 14 sts: 1 st remains on needle.

Change colors. Pick up 14 sts along left side of unit: 15 sts on the needle. Knit 9 rows, ending with a wrong-side row. BO 14 sts: 1 st remains on needle.

Pick up 19 sts along left side of unit: 20 sts on needle. Knit 9 rows, ending with a wrong-side row. BO 19 sts: 1 st remains on needle.

Change colors. Pick up 19 sts along left side of unit: 20 sts on needle. Knit 9 rows, ending with a right-side row. BO 19 sts: 1 st remains on needle.

Pick up 24 sts along left side of unit: 25 sts on needle. Knit 9 rows, ending with a wrong-side row. BO 24 sts: 1 st remains on needle.

Change colors. Pick up 24 sts along left side of unit: 25 sts on needle. Knit 9 rows, ending with a wrong-side row. BO 24 sts: 1 st remains on needle.

Pick up 29 sts along left side of unit: 30 sts on needle. Knit 9 rows, ending with a wrong-side row.

BO 29 sts: 1 st remains on needle.

Change colors. Pick up 29 sts along left side of unit: 30 sts on needle. Knit 9 rows, ending with a wrong-side row. BO 29 sts: 1 st remains on needle.

Pick up 34 sts along left side of unit: 35 sts on needle. Knit 9 rows, ending with a wrong-side row. BO all sts.

SIDE, BOTTOM AND STRAP

CO 10 sts. Knit until piece measures 105". BO.

FINISHING

To assemble bag sew four squares together into a larger square for the front of the bag. Repeat for the back.

Sew the two short ends of the strap together to form a large ring.

Sew the long edges of the strap to the sides and bottom of the front and back.

Fold the remaining part of the strap in half and sew the two long edges together to give the strap more strength. Don't be tempted to skip this stitch. The strap may flare and ruffle when felted if the edges are not sewn together.

FELT

Put the bag in a zippered pillow case to catch the lint, and toss it in the washing machine with an old towel or blue-jeans. Set the machine for the smallest load size with hot wash, cold rinse, and add a very small amount of soap.

Check the felting every few minutes. Some yarns and colors will felt within the first few minutes, while others may take two or three cycles.

When the fibers are matted and you don't want the bag to shrink any more, take it out and gently rinse in the sink. Roll the bag in a towel and squeeze out the excess water.

Don't panic if the bag looks lumpy or out of shape. The colors may not all felt equally. Pull on the bag to stretch it to the correct measurements and, if desired, put a cardboard box inside the bag to help keep it in shape while it dries. Leave to dry. Be patient, this may take a couple of days.

BUTTON AND LOOP

At center of back of the bag, 1" below top edge, pick up and knit 3 sts. You may need to use a knitting needle to poke a hole in the felt and a crochet hook to pull the yarn through. Knit for 3". BO. Sew the end of the loop to the picked up sts. Weave in ends.

Sew the button onto the center of the front of the bag 1" from the top.

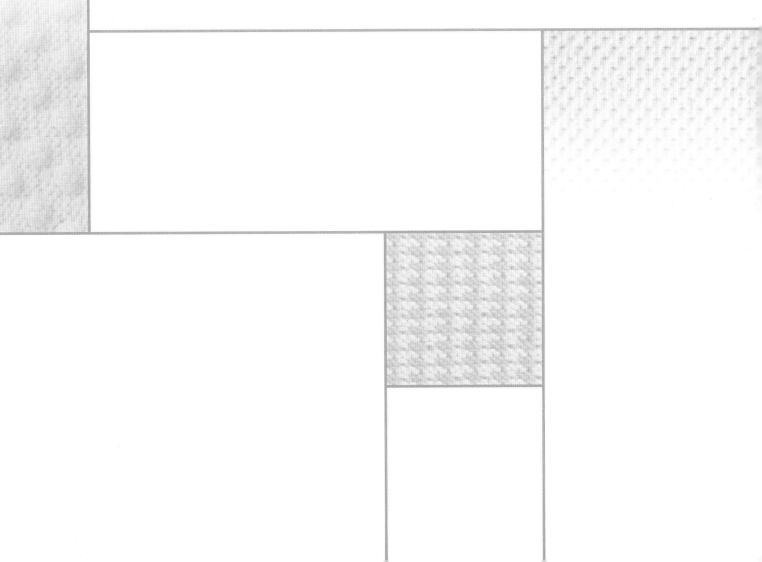

GARTER STITCHES

GARTER STITCHES

BEE

Multiple: 2 + 1

Stitch Guide

K1B (Knit 1 below): Insert needle into st below next st on left-hand needle and knit it, slipping the st above off the needle at the same time: K1B made.

INSTRUCTIONS

Row 1 (wrong side): Knit.

Row 2: K1; *K1B, K1; rep from * across.

Row 3: Knit.

Row 4: K2, K1B; *K1, K1B; rep from * to last 2 sts, K2.

Repeat Rows 1 through 4 for pattern.

BRICKS

Multiple: 4 + 3

Stitch Guide

YF: With yarn in front

INSTRUCTIONS

Row 1 (right side): K3; *sl 1, K3; rep from * to end.

Row 2: K3; *YF sl 1, K3; rep from * to end.

Row 3: K1, sl 1; *K3, sl 1; rep from * to last st, K1.

Row 4: K1, YF sl 1; *K3, YF sl 1; rep from * to last st, K1.

Repeat Rows 1 through 4 for pattern.

MOCK STOCKINETTE

Multiple: Any uneven number

Stitch Guide

K1B (Knit 1 below): Insert needle into st below next st on left-hand needle and knit it, slipping the st above off the needle at the same time: K1B made.

INSTRUCTIONS

Row 1: Knit.

Row 2 (right side): K1; *K1B, K1; rep from * to end.

Repeat Rows 1 and 2 for pattern.

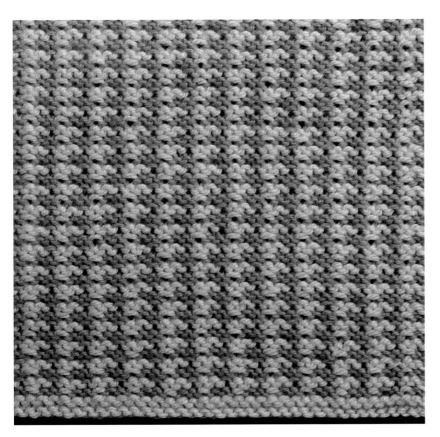

TWEED

Multiple: 3

Two Colors: Color A and Color B. Carry unused color loosely up the side.

INSTRUCTIONS

Rows 1 and 2: With Color A, knit.

Row 3 (right side): With Color B, *K2, sl 1; rep from * across.

Row 4: With Color B, knit.

Row 5: With Color A, *sl 1, K2; rep from * across.

Row 6: With Color A, knit.

Repeat Rows 3 through 6 for pattern.

BOBBLES

Multiple: 6 + 5

Stitch Guide

YB: With yarn in back

BB (Bobble): In next st work [(K1, YO) twice, K1], turn; YB, K5, turn; YB, K5, turn; YB, K2tog, K1, K2tog, turn; YB, sl 1, K2tog, PSSO: BB made.

INSTRUCTIONS

Rows 1 through 4: Knit.

Row 5: K5; *BB, K5; rep from * to end of row.

Rows 6 through 10: Knit.

Row 11: K2; *BB, K5; rep from *, ending last rep with K2.

Row 12: Knit.

Repeat Rows 1 through 12 for pattern.

LACE

Multiple: 3 + 2

INSTRUCTIONS

Row 1: Knit.

Row 2: K1; *K2tog, YO; rep from * to last 2 sts, K2.

Repeat Row 2 for pattern.

CHECKS

Multiple: 2 + 1

Stitch Guide

K1B (Knit 1 below): Insert needle into st below next st on left-hand needle and knit it, slipping the st above off the needle at the same time: K1B made.

Two colors: A and B. Carry unused color loosely up the side.

INSTRUCTIONS

Rows 1 and 2: With Color A, knit across.

Row 3 (right side): With color B, K1; *K1B, K1; rep from * across.

Row 4: With Color B, knit.

Row 5: With Color A, K2, K1B; *K1, K1B; rep from * across.

Row 6: With Color A, knit.

Repeat Rows 3 through 6 for pattern.

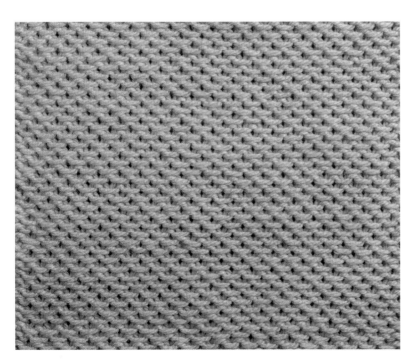

LOOP DE LOOP

Multiple: 2 + 2

INSTRUCTIONS

Row 1 (right side): Knit.

Row 2: *K1, sl 1; rep from * to last 2 sts, K2.

Row 3: Knit.

Row 4: K2; *sl 1, K1; rep from * across.

Repeat Rows 1 through 4 for pattern.

BERRIES

Multiple: 2 + 1

Stitch Guide

YB: With yarn in back

BB (Bobble): In next st work [(K1, YO) twice, K1], turn; YB, K5, turn; YB, K5, turn; YB, K2tog, K1, K2tog, turn; YB, sl 1, K2tog, PSSO: BB made.

INSTRUCTIONS:

Row 1 (right side): Knit.

Row 2: K1; *BB, K1; rep from * across.

Row 3: Knit.

Row 4: K2; *BB, K1; rep from * to last st, K1.

Repeat Rows 1 through 4 for pattern.

TEXTURE

Multiple: Any even number

INSTRUCTIONS

Row 1: Knit.

Row 2: K1; *YO, sl 1, K1, PSSO; rep from * to last st, K1.

Repeat Row 2 for pattern.

GRANITE

Multiple: 2

INSTRUCTIONS

Row 1 (wrong side): Knit.

Row 2: *K2tog; rep from * across.

Row 3: *Knit in front and back of stitch; rep from * across.

Row 4: Knit.

Repeat Rows 1 through 4 for pattern.

ZIGZAG

Multiple: 2 + 1

INSTRUCTIONS

Row 1 (right side): K1; *K2tog; rep from * across.

Row 2: K1; *YO, K1; rep from * across.

Row 3: *K2tog; rep from * to last st, K1.

Row 4: K1; *YO, K1; rep from * across.

Repeat Rows 1 through 4 for pattern.

EYELETS IN ROWS

Multiple: Any even number of sts

INSTRUCTIONS

Row 1: K1; *K2tog, YO; rep from * to last st, K1.

Row 2 (right side): Knit.

Row 3: K1; *YO, K2tog; rep from * to last st, K1.

Rows 4 through 6: Knit.

Row 7: K1; *YO, sl 1, K1, PSSO; rep from * to last st, K1.

Row 8: Knit.

Row 9: K1; *sl 1, K1, PSSO, YO; rep from * to last st, K1.

Rows 10 through 12: Knit.

Repeat Rows 1 through 12 for pattern.

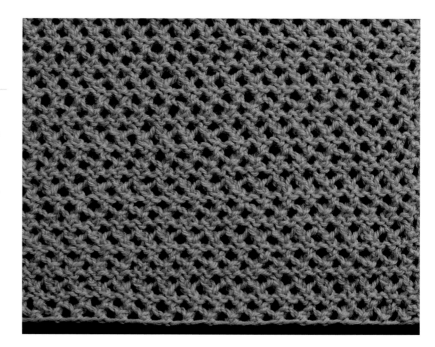

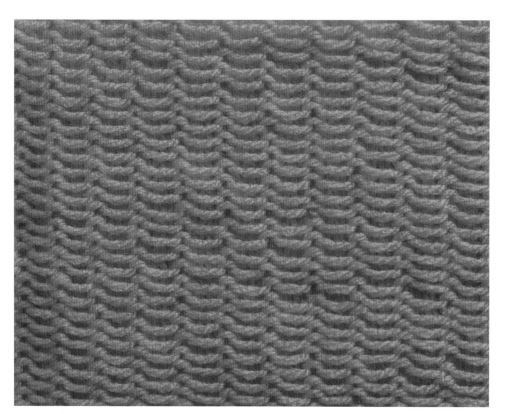

RUFFLES

Multiple: 3 + 2

Stitch Guide

YF: With yarn in front

YB: With yarn in back

INSTRUCTIONS

Note: Slip st through front lp from right to left.

Row 1: Knit.

Row 2 (right side): K1; *K1, YF sl 2 sts YB; rep from * to last st, K1.

Repeat Rows 1 and 2 for pattern.

MOSSY

Multiple: 2 + 1

Stitch Guide

YF: With yarn in front

INSTRUCTIONS

Row 1 (right side): K1; *sl 1, K1; rep from * to end.

Row 2: K1; *YF sl 1, K1; rep from * to end.

Row 3: K2; *sl 1, K1; rep from * to last st, K1.

Row 4: K2; *YF sl 1, K1; rep from * to last st, K1.

Repeat Rows 1 through 4 for pattern.

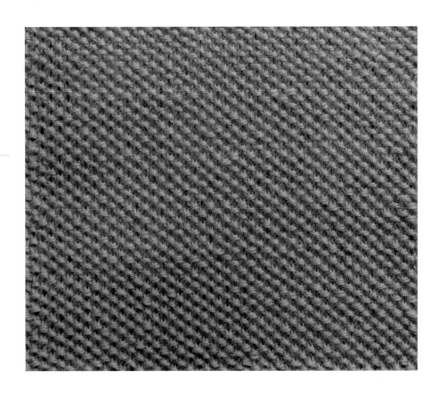

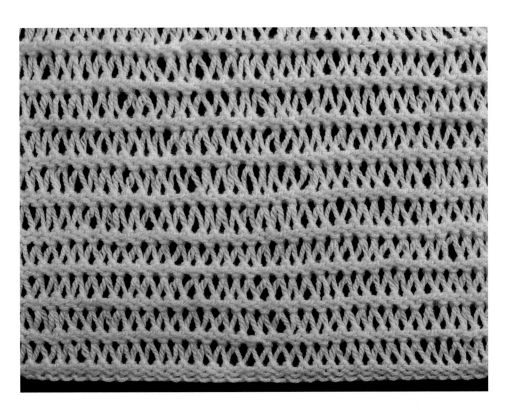

DROP STITCH

Multiple: Any number

INSTRUCTIONS

Row 1 (right side): Knit.

Row 2: Knit.

Row 3: *K1, (YO) twice; rep from * across.

Row 4: Knit, dropping the extra lps.

Repeat Rows 1 through 4 for pattern.

CLOVERS

Multiple: 4 + 3

Stitch Guide

YB: With yarn in back

Two Colors: Color A and Color B

INSTRUCTIONS

Note: Slip st through front lp.

Row 1: With A, K3, *YB, sl 1, K3; rep from * across.

Row 2: With A, knit.

Row 3: With B, K1, *YB, sl 1, K3; rep from * to last 3 sts, YB, sl 1, K1.

Row 4: With B, knit.

Repeat Rows 1 through 4 for pattern.

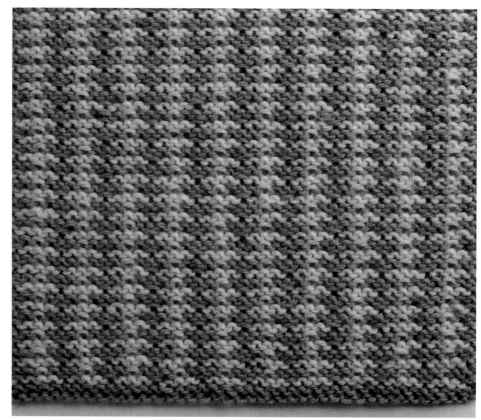

STAR STITCH

Multiple: 3

Two Colors: Color A and Color B. Carry unused color loosely up the side.

INSTRUCTIONS

Row 1 (right side): With Color A, knit.

Row 2: With Color A, K2; *YO, sl 1, K2, pass sl st over 2 knit sts; rep from * to last st, K1.

Row 3: With Color B, knit.

Row 4: With Color B, K1; *sl 1, K2, pass sl st over 2 knit sts, YO; rep from * to last two sts, K2.

Repeat Rows 1 through 4 for pattern.

HALF BRIOCHE

Multiple: Any even number

Stitch Guide

K1B (Knit 1 below): Insert needle into st below next st on left-hand needle and knit it, slipping the st above off the needle at the same time: K1B made.

INSTRUCTIONS

Row 1: Knit.

Row 2 (right side): K1; *K1, K1B; rep from * to last st, K1.

Row 3: Knit.

Row 4: K1; *K1B, K1; rep from * to last st, K1.

Repeat Rows 1 through 4 for pattern.

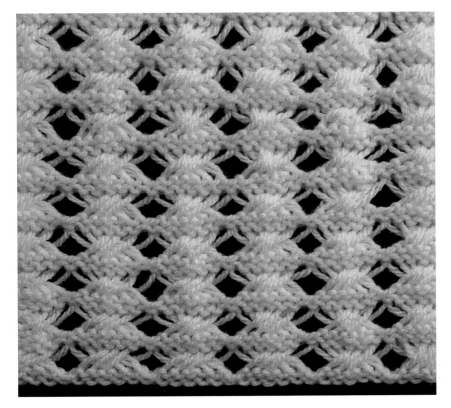

ELONGATED CROSS OVER

Multiple: 6 + 2

INSTRUCTIONS

Row 1 (right side): Knit.

Row 2: K1; *K1, (YO) 3 times; rep from * to last st, K1.

Row 3: K1; *Sl 6 sts to right-hand needle allowing YO's to drop from needle: 6 long sts. Sl long sts to left needle. Reaching needle in front of first 3 sts, knit 4th, 5th and 6th sts. Then knit skipped 1st, 2nd and 3rd sts; rep from * to last st, K1.

Row 4: Knit.

Repeat Rows 1 through 4 for pattern.

CONTRARY BRIOCHE

Multiple: 2 + 2

Stitch Guide

K1B (Knit 1 below): Insert needle into st below next st on left-hand needle and knit it, slipping the st above off the needle at the same time: K1B made.

INSTRUCTIONS

Row 1 : Knit.

Row 2 (right side): K1; *K1, K1B; rep from * to last st, K1.

Rows 3 through 5: Rep Row 2.

Row 6: K1; *K1B, K1; rep from * to last st, K1.

Rows 7 through 9: Rep Row 6.

Repeat Rows 2 through 9 for pattern.

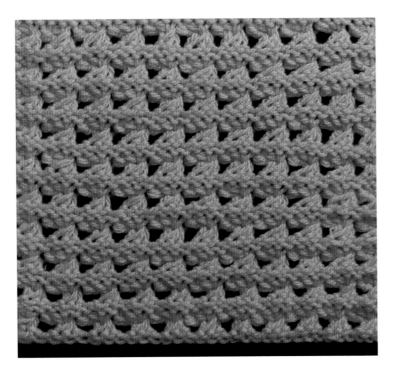

ENCHANTING EYELETS

Multiple: 3 + 2

INSTRUCTIONS

Row 1 (right side): Knit.

Row 2: K1; *(YO) three times, K1; rep from * to last 2 sts, (YO) three times, K2.

Row 3: K1; *(sl 1, dropping 3 YO's) 3 times: 3 long sts. Sl 3 long sts to left needle. Knit them tog tbl, then knit tog through front lp, and finally knit tog through back lp; rep from * to last st, K1.

Row 4: Knit.

Repeat Rows 1 through 4 for pattern.

FURLS

Multiple: Any even number

INSTRUCTIONS

Row 1: K1; *YO, K2tog; rep from * to last st, K1.

Row 2 (right side): Knit across.

Repeat Rows 1 and 2 for pattern.

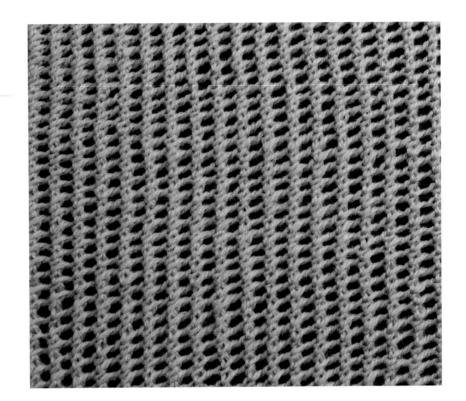

BABY EYELETS

Multiple: Any odd number

INSTRUCTIONS

Rows 1 through 3: Knit.

Row 4 (right side): K1; *K2tog, YO; rep from * to last 2 sts, K2.

Rows 5 through 7: Knit.

Row 8 (right side): K1; *K1, YO; rep from * to last 2 sts, K2.

Row 9: K1; *K1, drop YO; rep from * to last 2 sts, K2.

Row 10: Knit.

Repeat Rows 1 through 10 for pattern.

LINEN

Multiple: 6

Stitch Guide

YF: With yarn in front

YB: With yarn in back

Two colors: color A and Color B

INSTRUCTIONS

Row 1 (right side): With Color A, knit.

Row 2: With Color B, K3; *YF, sl 1, K5; rep from * to last 3 sts, YF, sl 1, K2.

Row 3: With Color B, K2; *YB, sl 1, K5; rep from * to last 4 sts, YB, sl 1, K3.

Row 4: With Color A, *YF, sl 1, K1; rep from * across.

Row 5: With Color A, *K1, YB, sl 2; rep from * across.

Repeat Rows 2 through 5 for pattern.

RIBS

Multiple: 3 + 1

INSTRUCTIONS

Note: Slip st through front lp from right to left.

Row 1 (right side): Sl 1; *K2tog, YO, sl 1; rep from * to last 3 sts, K2tog, K1.

Row 2: Sl 1; *YO, sl 1, K2tog; rep to last 2 sts, YO, sl 1, K1.

Repeat Rows 1 and 2 for pattern.

KNOBBIES

Multiple: 4 + 2

Stitch Guide

KN Knob: (K1, YO, pass knit st over YO and return to left needle) 3 times, leaving last YO on right needle.

Three Colors: Color A, Color B and Color C

INSTRUCTIONS:

Row 1 (right side): With A, knit.

Row 2: With A, knit.

Row 3: With A, K2; *with B, work KN, with A, K1; rep from *.

Row 4: With A, knit.

Row 5: *With A, K1, with C, work KN; rep from * to last 2 sts, with A, K2.

Row 6: With A, knit.

Repeat Rows 3 through 6 for pattern. Weave in ends.

CORRUGATED

Multiple: 3 + 2

INSTRUCTIONS

Note: Slip st through front lp from right to left.

Row 1 (right side): Knit.

Row 2: K1; *K1, sl 2; rep from * to last st, K1.

Repeat Rows 1 and 2 for pattern.

SLANTING BOBBLES

Multiple: 5 + 2

Stitch Guide

BB (Bobble): In next st work [(K1, YO) twice, K1], turn; YB, K5, turn; YB, K5, turn; YB, K2tog, K1, K2tog, turn; YB, sl 1, K2tog, PSSO: BB made.

YB: With yarn in back

INSTRUCTIONS

Row 1 (right side): K5, BB, *K4, BB; rep from * to last st, K1.

Row 2 and all even rows: Knit.

Row 3: *K4; BB; rep from * to last 2 sts, K2.

Row 5: K3, BB, *K4, BB; rep from * to last 3 sts, K3.

Row 7: K2; *BB, K4; rep from * across.

Row 9: K1; *BB, K4; rep from * to last st, K1.

Repeat Rows 1 through 10 for pattern.

BRIOCHE RIB

Multiple: 2 sts

Stitch Guide

K1B (Knit 1 below): Insert needle into st below next st on left-hand needle and knit it, slipping the st above off the needle at the same time: K1B made.

INSTRUCTIONS

Row 1: Knit.

Row 2: *K1, K1B; rep from * to last 2 sts, K2.

Repeat Row 2 for pattern.

PLAID

Multiple: 8 + 6

Stitch Guide

KW: Knit 1, wrapping yarn twice around needle.

YF: With yarn in front

YB: With yarn in back

Two colors: Color A and Color B.

INSTRUCTIONS

Note: Slip st through front lp from right to left.

Row 1 (right side): With A, Knit.

Row 2: Rep Row 1.

Row 3: With B, K1, sl 1, K2, sl 1; *K4, sl 1, K2, sl 1; rep from * to last st, K1.

Row 4: With B, K1, YF, sl 1, YB, K2, YF, sl 1, *YB, K4, YF, sl 1, YB, K2, YF, sl 1; rep from * to last st, YB, K1.

Row 5: With A, Knit.

Row 6: With A, K1, KW, K2, KW; *K4, KW, K2, KW; rep from * to last st, K1.

Row 7: With B, K1, sl 1, allowing lp to drop, K2, sl 1, allowing lp to drop, ; *K4, sl 1, allowing lp to drop, K2, sl 1, allowing lp to drop; rep from * to last st, K1.

Row 8: Rep Row 4.

Row 9: Rep Row 3.

Row 10: Rep Row 4.

Row 11: Rep Row 3.

Row 12: Rep Row 4.

Repeat Rows 1 through 12 for pattern.

WOVEN CABLES

Multiple: 12 + 2

Stitch Guide

KW: K1, wrapping yarn 3 times around needle.

K6B: Sl 3 sts to cable needle and hold in back; K3, K3 from cable needle.

K6F: Sl 3 sts from cable needle and hold in front; K3, K3 frm cable needle.

INSTRUCTIONS

Row 1 (right side): Knit.

Row 2: K1; *KW; rep from * to last st, K1.

Row 3: K1; *sl 6 sts to right-hand needle, dropping lps; sl 6 sts back to left-hand needle, K6B; rep from * to last st, K1.

Row 4: Knit.

Row 5: Knit.

Row 6: K4; *KW; rep from * to last 4 sts, K4.

Row 7: K4; *sl 6 sts to right hand-needle, dropping lps;

sl 6 sts back to left-hand needle, K6F; rep from * to last 4 sts, K4.

Row 8: Knit.

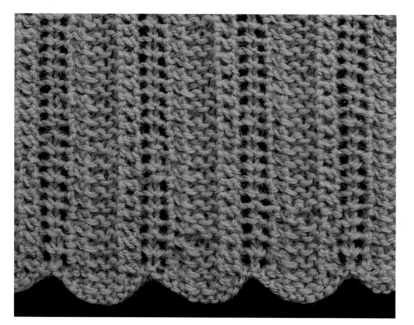

PEAKS AND VALLEYS

Multiple: 11 + 2

INSTRUCTIONS

Row 1: Knit.

Row 2 (right side): K1; *(K2tog) twice, (YO, K1) three times, YO, (K2tog) twice; rep from * to last st; K1.

Repeat Rows 1 and 2 for pattern.

GENERAL DIRECTIONS

Abbreviations and Symbols

Knit patterns are written in a special shorthand, which is used so that instructions don't take up too much space. They sometimes seem confusing, but once you learn them, you'll have no trouble following them.

These are Standard Abbreviations

Beg . . . . beginning

BB . . . . bobble

BO . . . . bind off

CC. . . . . contrast color

CO. cast on

DD. . . . . double decrease

Dec . . . . decrease

Fig . . . . figure

Inc. . . . . increase(ing)

K. . . . . knit

K1B . . . . knit 1 st in row below

K2tog. . . knit two stitches together

Lp(s). . . . . loop(s)

M1 . . . . Increase one stitch

MC . . . . main color

Mm . . . . millimeter(s)

Oz . . . . ounces

Patt . . . . pattern

PM. . . . . place marker

Prev . . . . previous

PS. . . . . pass picked up st over

PSSO. . . pass the slipped stitch over

P2SSO. . pass 2 slipped stitches over

PU . . . . . . pick up and knit 1 stitch

Rem . . . . remain(ing)

Rep . . . . repeat(ing)

Sk. . . . . skip

Sl . . . . slip

Sl 1K . . . . slip 1 stitch with
yarn in back

Sl 1P. . . . . slip 1 stitch with
yarn in front

SM . . . . slip marker

SSK . . . . slip, slip, knit

St(s) . . . . stitch(es)

Tbl. . . . . through back loop

Tog. . . . . together

YB. . . . with yarn in back of needle

YF. . . . with yarn in front of needle

YO . . . . Yarn over the needle

YRN . . . . Yarn around needle

These are Standard Symbols

* An asterisk (or double asterisks**) in a pattern row, indicates a portion of instructions to be used more than once. For instance, "rep from * three times" means that after working the instructions once, you must work them again three times for a total of 4 times in all.

† A dagger (or double daggers ††) indicates that those instructions will be repeated again later in the same row or round.

: The number after a colon tells you the number of stitches you will have when you have completed the row or round.

( ) Parentheses enclose instructions which are to be worked the number of times following the parentheses. For instance, "(K1, P2) 3 times" means that you knit one stitch and then purl two stitches, three times.

Parentheses often set off or clarify a group of stitches to be worked into the same space or stitch.

[ ] Brackets and ( ) parentheses are also used to give you additional information. For instance, "(rem sts are left unworked)"

Terms

Finish off—This means to end your piece by pulling the yarn through the last loop remaining on the needle. This will prevent the work from unraveling.

Continue in Pattern as Established—This means to follow the pattern stitch as if has been set up, working any increases or decreases in such a way that the pattern remains the same as it was established.

Work even—This means that the work is continued in the pattern as established without increasing or decreasing.

Right Side—This means the side of the garment that will be seen.

Wrong Side—This means the side of the garment that is inside when the garment is worn.

Right Front—This means the part of the garment that will be worn on the right side of the body.

Left Front—This means the part of the garment that will be worn on the left side of the body.

GENERAL DIRECTIONS

Gauge

This is probably the most important aspect of knitting!

GAUGE simply means the number of stitches per inch, and the numbers of rows per inch that result from a specified yarn worked with needles in a specified size. But since everyone knits —some loosely, some tightly, some in-between—the measurements of individual work can vary greatly, even when the knitters use the same pattern and the same size yarn and or needle.

If you don't work to the gauge specified in the pattern, your project will never be the correct size, and you may not have enough yarn to finish your project. Needle sizes given in instructions are merely guides, and should never be used without a gauge swatch.

To make a gauge swatch, knit a swatch that is about 4" square, using the suggested needle and the number of stitches given in the pattern. Measure your swatch. If the number of stitches is fewer than those listed in the pattern, try making another swatch with a smaller needle. If the number of stitches is more than is called for in the pattern, try making another swatch with a larger needle. It is your responsibility to make sure you achieve the gauge specified in the pattern.

3-Needle Bind-off

Hold right side of both pieces together with both needles pointing to the right.

*Insert the 3rd needle through the first stitch on both needles and knit them together. Place the new stitch on the 3rd needle. Repeat the procedure again. Pass the first stitch over the second one. Repeat from * until all stitches are bound off.

Metric Equivalents					
inches	cm	inches	cm	inches	cm
1	2.54	11	27.94	21	53.34
2	5.08	12	30.48	22	55.88
3	7.62	13	33.02	23	58.42
4	10.16	14	35.56	24	60.96
5	12.70	15	38.10	30	76.20
6	15.24	16	40.64	36	91.44
7	17.78	17	43.18	42	106.68
8	20.32	18	45.72	48	121.92
9	22.86	19	48.26	54	137.16
10	25.40	20	50.80	60	152.40

The patterns in this book have been written using the knitting terminology that is used in the United States. Terms which may have different equivalents in other parts of the world are listed below.

United States	International
Gauge	tension
Skip	miss
Yarn over (YO)	yarn forward (yfwd)
Bind off	Cast off

Knitting Needles Conversion Chart

U.S.	0	1	2	3	4	5	6	7	8	9	10	10½	11	13	15	17
Metric	2	2.25	2.75	3.25	3.5	3.75	4	4.5	5	5.5	6	6.5	8	9	10	12.75

ACKNOWLEDGMENTS

Whenever we have used a special yarn we have given the brand name. If you are unable to find these yarns locally, write to the following manufacturers who will be able to tell you where to purchase their products, or consult their internet sites. We also wish to thank these companies for supplying yarn for this book.

Bernat Yarns
320 Livingston Avenue South
Listowel, Ontario
Canada N4W 3H3
www.bernat.com

Berroco, Inc.
14 Elmdale Road
Uxbridge, Massachusetts 01569
www.berroco.com

Cherry Tree Hill
100 Cherry Tree Hill Ln
Barton, Vermont 05822
www.cherryyarn.com

Crystal Palace Yarns
160 23rd Street
Richmond, California 94804
www.straw.com

Jelly Yarns
P. O. Box 543
Southampton, Pennsylvania 18966
www.3dimillus.com

S. R. Kertzer Limited
50 Trowers Rd
Woodbridge Ontario L4L 7K6
Canada
www.kertzer.com

Lion Brand Yarn
135 Kero Road
Carlstadt, New Jersey 07072
www.lionbrand.com

Patons Yarns
2700 Dufferin Street
Toronto, Ontario
Canada M6B 4J3
www.patonsyarns.com

Plymouth Yarn Co., Inc
500 Lafayette Street
P.O. Box 28
Bristol, Pennsylvania 19007-0028
www.plymouthyarn.com

Prism Arts, Inc.
3140 39th Ave N
St. Petersburg, Florida 33714-4530
www.prismyarn.com

Red Heart Yarns
Coats and Clark
Consumer Services
P. O. Box 12229
Greenville, South Carolina 29612-0229
www.coatsandclark.com

Rowan Yarns
18 Celina Avenue #17
Nashua, New Hampshire 03063
www.westminsterfibers.com

Sirdar Yarn
Knitting Fever
315 Bayview Avenue
Amityville, New York 11701
www.knittingfever.com

Tahki Stacy Charles, Inc.
70-30 80th Street
  Bldg 36
Ridgewood, New York 11385
www.tahkistacycharles.com

The authors thank the following contributing designers:

Valentina Devine,
Los Alamos, New Mexico

Donna Druchunas,
Longmont, Colorado

Nazanin S. Fard,
Novato, California

Kathleen Greco,
Southampton, Pennsylvania

Rebecca Hatcher,
Andover, Massachusetts

Rosalie Johnston,
Southampton, Pennsylvania

Jodi Lewanda,
Farmington, Connecticut

Diane Moyer,
Orange, Connecticut

Joyce Renee Wyatt,
Los Angeles, California

INDEX